SECRET

RESTAURANT

RECIPES | *the ultimate collection*

Publications International, Ltd.

Photograph on page 37 © Shutterstock.com.

Pictured on the front cover *(clockwise from top left):* Potato Skins *(page 40)* Guacamole Burgers *(page 146)*, Garlic Knots *(page 242)*, Marbled Cookie Brownie *(page 266)*, Chocolate Frosty *(page 299)*, Pasta Campagnolo *(page 208)* and Roasted Brussels Sprouts Salad *(page 138)*.

Pictured on the back cover *(clockwise from bottom):* Double Chocolate Cookies and Cream Mousse *(page 282)*, Chicken Burrito Bowls *(page 186)*, Barbecue Chicken Pizza *(page 179)*, Amazing Apple Salad *(page 136)* and Chicken Parmesan Sliders**.**

ISBN: 978-1-64558-732-3

Manufactured in China.

8 7 6 5 4 3 2 1

Microwave Cooking: Microwave ovens vary in wattage. Use the cooking times as guidelines and check for doneness before adding more time.

Note: This book was not licensed or endorsed by and is not affiliated with or approved by any of the owners of the trademarks or brand names referred to in the book.

WARNING: Food preparation, baking and cooking involve inherent dangers: misuse of electric products, sharp electric tools, boiling water, hot stoves, allergic reactions, foodborne illnesses and the like, pose numerous potential risks. Publications International, Ltd. (PIL) assumes no responsibility or liability for any damages you may experience as a result of following recipes, instructions, tips or advice in this publication.

While we hope this publication helps you find new ways to eat delicious foods, you may not always achieve the results desired due to variations in ingredients, cooking temperatures, typos, errors, omissions, or individual cooking abilities.

Let's get social!
⬭ @Publications_International
⬤ @PublicationsInternational
www.pilbooks.com

STRAWBERRY-TOPPED PANCAKES *(page 24)*

GARDEN VEGETABLE SOUP *(page 96)*

DOUBLE DECKER TACOS *(page 154)*

contents

breakfast & brunch

INSPIRED BY
THE ORIGINAL®
PANCAKE
HOUSE

DUTCH BABY PANCAKE

MAKES 2 SERVINGS

3 tablespoons butter, divided, plus additional for serving

½ cup all-purpose flour

2 tablespoons granulated sugar

¼ teaspoon salt

½ cup whole milk, at room temperature

2 eggs, at room temperature

¼ teaspoon vanilla

Powdered sugar

Lemon wedges

1. Preheat oven to 400°F. Place 1 tablespoon butter in 9- to 10-inch ovenproof skillet; place skillet in oven to heat while preparing batter. Melt remaining 2 tablespoons butter in small bowl; let cool slightly.

2. Combine flour, granulated sugar and salt in medium bowl; mix well. Add milk, eggs, melted butter and vanilla; whisk 1 minute or until batter is very smooth.

3. Remove skillet from oven; immediately pour batter into hot skillet.

4. Bake about 20 minutes or until outside of pancake is puffed and edges are deep golden brown. Sprinkle with powdered sugar; serve with lemon wedges and additional butter.

RICH AND GOOEY CINNAMON BUNS

MAKES 12 BUNS

DOUGH

- 1 package (¼ ounce) active dry yeast
- 1 cup warm milk (110°F)
- 2 eggs, beaten
- ½ cup granulated sugar
- ¼ cup (½ stick) butter, softened
- 1 teaspoon salt
- 4 to 4¼ cups all-purpose flour

FILLING

- 1 cup packed brown sugar
- 3 tablespoons ground cinnamon

  Pinch salt
- 6 tablespoons (¾ stick) butter, softened

ICING

- 1½ cups powdered sugar
- 3 ounces cream cheese, softened
- ¼ cup (½ stick) butter, softened
- ½ teaspoon vanilla
- ⅛ teaspoon salt

1. Dissolve yeast in warm milk in large bowl of electric stand mixer. Add eggs, granulated sugar, ¼ cup butter and 1 teaspoon salt; beat with paddle attachment at medium speed until well blended. Add 4 cups flour; beat at low speed until dough begins to come together. Knead dough with dough hook at low speed about 5 minutes or until dough is smooth, elastic and slightly sticky. Add additional flour, 1 tablespoon at a time, if necessary to prevent sticking.

2. Shape dough into a ball. Place in large greased bowl; turn to grease top. Cover and let rise in warm place about 1 hour or until doubled in size. Meanwhile, for filling, combine brown sugar, cinnamon and pinch of salt in small bowl; mix well.

3. Spray 13×9-inch baking pan with nonstick cooking spray. Roll out dough into 18×14-inch rectangle on floured surface. Spread 6 tablespoons butter evenly over dough; top with cinnamon-sugar mixture.

4. Beginning with long side, roll up dough tightly jelly-roll style; pinch seam to seal. Cut log crosswise into 12 slices; place slices cut sides up in prepared pan. Cover and let rise in warm place about 30 minutes or until almost doubled in size. Preheat oven to 350°F.

5. Bake 20 to 25 minutes or until golden brown. Meanwhile, prepare icing. Combine powdered sugar, cream cheese, ¼ cup butter, vanilla and ⅛ teaspoon salt in medium bowl; beat with electric mixer at medium speed 2 minutes or until smooth and creamy. Spread icing generously over warm cinnamon buns.

SWEET POTATO PANCAKES

MAKES 5 SERVINGS (10 LARGE PANCAKES)

PANCAKES

- 2 medium sweet potatoes
- 2½ cups all-purpose flour
- 1 teaspoon baking powder
- 1 teaspoon baking soda
- ½ teaspoon salt
- ½ teaspoon ground cinnamon
- ¼ teaspoon ground ginger
- 2¾ cups buttermilk
- 2 eggs
- 2 tablespoons packed brown sugar
- 2 tablespoons butter, melted and cooled, plus additional for pan

GINGER BUTTER

- ¼ cup (½ stick) butter, softened
- 1 tablespoon packed brown sugar
- 1 teaspoon grated fresh ginger
- Pinch salt
- Prepared caramel sauce or maple syrup
- ¾ cup chopped glazed pecans*

*Glazed or candied pecans may be found in the produce section of the supermarket along with other salad convenience items, or they may be found in the snack aisle.

1. Preheat oven to 375°F. Scrub sweet potatoes; bake 50 to 60 minutes or until soft. Cool slightly; peel and mash. Measure out 1⅓ cups for pancake batter.

2. Combine flour, baking powder, baking soda, salt, cinnamon and ground ginger in medium bowl; mix well. Whisk buttermilk, eggs and 2 tablespoons brown sugar in large bowl until well blended. Stir in 2 tablespoons melted butter. Add sweet potatoes; whisk until well blended. Add flour mixture; stir just until dry ingredients are moistened and no streaks of flour remain. Do not overmix; batter will be lumpy. Let stand 10 minutes.

3. Heat griddle or large skillet* over medium heat; brush with butter to coat. For each pancake, pour ½ cup of batter onto griddle, spreading into 5- to 6-inch circle. Cook about 4 minutes or until bottom is golden brown and small bubbles appear on surface. Turn pancake; cook about 3 minutes or until golden brown. Add additional butter to griddle as needed.

4. For ginger butter, beat ¼ cup softened butter, 1 tablespoon brown sugar, fresh ginger and pinch of salt in small bowl until well blended. If using caramel sauce, microwave according to package directions. Stir in water, 1 teaspoon at a time, to thin to desired pouring consistency.

5. Serve pancakes warm topped with ginger butter, caramel sauce and glazed pecans.

*Since pancakes are large, a skillet may not be able to cook more than one at a time. Keep pancakes warm in 250°F oven on wire rack set over baking sheet.

SPINACH ARTICHOKE EGG SOUFFLÉS

MAKES 8 SERVINGS

1 package (about 17 ounces) frozen puff pastry (2 sheets), thawed

1 teaspoon olive oil

¼ cup chopped onion

1 clove garlic, minced

¼ cup finely chopped roasted red pepper (1 pepper)

¼ cup finely chopped canned artichoke hearts (about 2 medium)

¼ cup frozen chopped spinach, thawed and squeezed dry

3 eggs, separated

½ (8-ounce) package cream cheese, softened

½ teaspoon salt

⅛ teaspoon black pepper

4 tablespoons grated Romano cheese, divided

1. Preheat oven to 400°F. Spray eight 4-inch or 1-cup ramekins or jumbo (3½-inch) muffin pan cups with nonstick cooking spray. Unfold puff pastry; cut each sheet into quarters. Gently press each pastry square into bottoms and partially up sides of prepared ramekins. (Pastry should not reach tops of ramekins.) Place ramekins on baking sheet; refrigerate while preparing filling.

2. Heat oil in medium skillet over medium heat. Add onion; cook and stir 2 minutes or until softened and lightly browned. Add garlic; cook and stir 30 seconds. Add roasted pepper, artichokes and spinach; cook and stir 2 minutes or until liquid has evaporated.

3. Whisk egg yolks, cream cheese, salt and black pepper in medium bowl until well blended. Stir in vegetable mixture and 3 tablespoons Romano cheese.

4. Beat egg whites in large bowl with electric mixer at high speed 3 minutes or until stiff peaks form. Fold into vegetable mixture until blended. Divide mixture evenly among pastry-lined ramekins; sprinkle with remaining 1 tablespoon Romano cheese. Fold corners of pastry towards center.

5. Bake 25 minutes or until crust is golden brown and filling is puffed. Cool in ramekins 2 minutes; remove to wire rack. Serve warm.

STRAWBERRY BANANA FRENCH TOAST

MAKES 2 SERVINGS

INSPIRED
BY IHOP®

- 1 cup sliced fresh strawberries (about 8 medium)
- 2 teaspoons sugar
- 2 eggs
- ½ cup milk
- 3 tablespoons all-purpose flour
- 1 teaspoon vanilla
- ⅛ teaspoon salt
- 1 tablespoon butter
- 4 slices (1 inch thick) egg bread or country bread
- 1 banana, cut into ¼-inch slices

  Whipped cream and powdered sugar (optional)

  Maple syrup

1. Combine strawberries and sugar in small bowl; toss to coat. Set aside while preparing French toast.

2. Whisk eggs, milk, flour, vanilla and salt in shallow bowl or pie plate until well blended. Melt ½ tablespoon butter in large skillet over medium-high heat. Working with two slices at a time, dip bread into egg mixture, turning to coat completely; let excess drip off. Add to skillet; cook 3 to 4 minutes per side or until golden brown. Repeat with remaining butter and bread slices.

3. Top each serving with strawberry mixture and banana slices. Garnish with whipped cream and powdered sugar; serve with maple syrup.

CINNAMON SWIRL COFFEECAKE

MAKES 9 TO 12 SERVINGS

FILLING AND TOPPING

- ⅓ cup all-purpose flour
- ⅓ cup granulated sugar
- ⅓ cup packed brown sugar
- 1½ tablespoons ground cinnamon
- ¼ teaspoon salt
- ⅛ teaspoon ground allspice
- 3 tablespoons melted butter

CAKE

- 2 cups all-purpose flour
- 1½ teaspoons baking powder
- ¾ teaspoon baking soda
- ½ teaspoon salt
- 9 tablespoons butter, softened
- 1¼ cups granulated sugar
- 3 eggs
- ½ cup sour cream
- 2 teaspoons vanilla
- ¾ cup milk

1. Preheat oven to 350°F. Spray 9-inch square baking pan with nonstick cooking spray.

2. For filling, combine ⅓ cup flour, ⅓ cup granulated sugar, brown sugar, cinnamon, ¼ teaspoon salt and allspice in small bowl; mix well. For topping, remove half of mixture to another small bowl; stir in melted butter until blended.

3. For cake, combine 2 cups flour, baking powder, baking soda and ½ teaspoon salt in medium bowl; mix well. Combine 9 tablespoons butter and 1¼ cups granulated sugar in large bowl; beat with electric mixer at medium speed 3 minutes or until light and fluffy. Add eggs, sour cream and vanilla; beat until well blended. Scrape down side of bowl. Add flour mixture alternately with milk in two additions, beating at low speed until blended. Spread half of batter in prepared pan; sprinkle evenly with filling. Spread remaining batter over filling with dampened hands. Sprinkle with topping.

4. Bake 45 to 50 minutes or until toothpick inserted into center comes out clean. Cool completely in pan on wire rack.

STUFFED HASH BROWNS

MAKES 1 TO 2 SERVINGS

1½ cups shredded potatoes*

2 tablespoons finely chopped onion

¼ plus ⅛ teaspoon salt, divided

⅛ teaspoon black pepper

2 tablespoons butter, divided

1 tablespoon vegetable oil

½ cup diced ham (¼-inch pieces)

3 eggs

2 tablespoons milk

2 slices American cheese

Use refrigerated shredded hash brown potatoes or shredded peeled russet potatoes, squeezed dry.

1. Preheat oven to 250°F. Place wire rack over baking sheet. Combine potatoes, onion, ¼ teaspoon salt and pepper in medium bowl; mix well.

2. Heat 1 tablespoon butter and oil in small (6- to 8-inch) nonstick skillet over medium heat. Add potato mixture; spread to cover bottom of skillet evenly, pressing down gently with spatula to flatten. Cook about 10 minutes or until bottom and edges are golden brown. Cover skillet with large inverted plate; carefully flip hash browns onto plate. Slide hash browns back into skillet, cooked side up. Cook 10 minutes or until golden brown. Slide hash browns onto prepared wire rack; place in oven to keep warm while preparing ham and eggs.

3. Melt 1 teaspoon butter in same skillet over medium-high heat. Add ham; cook and stir 2 to 3 minutes or until lightly browned. Remove to plate.

4. Whisk eggs, milk and remaining ⅛ teaspoon salt in small bowl. Melt remaining 2 teaspoons butter in same skillet over medium-high heat. Add egg mixture; cook about 3 minutes or just until eggs are cooked through, stirring to form large, fluffy curds. Place cheese slices on top of eggs; remove from heat and cover skillet with lid or foil to melt cheese.

5. Cut hash browns in half. Place one half on serving plate; sprinkle with ham. Top with eggs and remaining half of hash browns.

/ /

tip

Refrigerated shredded potatoes are very wet when removed from the package. For the best results, dry them well with paper towels before cooking.

BAKED APPLE PANCAKE

MAKES 2 TO 4 SERVINGS

- 3 tablespoons butter
- 3 medium Granny Smith apples (about 1¼ pounds), peeled and cut into ¼-inch slices
- ½ cup packed dark brown sugar
- 1½ teaspoons ground cinnamon
- ½ teaspoon plus pinch of salt, divided
- 4 eggs
- ⅓ cup whipping cream
- ⅓ cup milk
- 2 tablespoons granulated sugar
- ½ teaspoon vanilla
- ⅔ cup all-purpose flour

1. Melt butter in 8-inch ovenproof nonstick or cast iron skillet over medium heat. Add apples, brown sugar, cinnamon and pinch of salt; cook 8 minutes or until apples begin to soften, stirring occasionally. Spread apples in even layer in skillet; set aside to cool 30 minutes.

2. After apples have cooled 30 minutes, preheat oven to 425°F. Whisk eggs in large bowl until foamy. Add cream, milk, granulated sugar, vanilla and remaining ½ teaspoon salt; whisk until blended. Sift flour into egg mixture; whisk until batter is well blended and smooth. Set aside 15 minutes.

3. Stir batter; pour evenly over apple mixture. Place skillet on rimmed baking sheet in case of drips (or place baking sheet or piece of foil in oven beneath skillet).

4. Bake 16 minutes or until top is golden brown and pancake is loose around edge. Cool 1 minute; loosen edge of pancake with spatula, if necessary. Place large serving plate or cutting board on top of skillet and invert pancake onto plate. Serve warm.

FRITTATA RUSTICA

MAKES 2 SERVINGS

4 ounces cremini mushrooms, stems trimmed, cut into thirds

1 tablespoon olive oil, divided

½ teaspoon plus ⅛ teaspoon salt, divided

½ cup chopped onion

1 cup packed chopped stemmed lacinato kale

½ cup halved grape tomatoes

4 eggs

½ teaspoon Italian seasoning

Black pepper

⅓ cup shredded mozzarella cheese

1 tablespoon shredded Parmesan cheese

Chopped fresh parsley (optional)

1. Preheat oven to 400°F. Spread mushrooms on small baking sheet; drizzle with 1 teaspoon oil and sprinkle with ⅛ teaspoon salt. Roast 15 to 20 minutes or until well browned and tender.

2. Heat remaining 2 teaspoons oil in small (6- to 8-inch) nonstick skillet over medium heat. Add onion; cook and stir 5 minutes or until soft. Add kale and ¼ teaspoon salt; cook and stir 10 minutes or until kale is tender. Add tomatoes; cook and stir 3 minutes or until tomatoes are soft. Stir in mushrooms.

3. Preheat broiler. Whisk eggs, remaining ¼ teaspoon salt, Italian seasoning and pepper in small bowl until well blended.

4. Pour egg mixture over vegetables in skillet; stir gently to mix. Cook about 3 minutes or until eggs are set around edge, lifting edge to allow uncooked portion to flow underneath. Sprinkle with mozzarella and Parmesan. Broil 3 minutes or until eggs are set and cheese is browned. Garnish with parsley.

INSPIRED BY
WAFFLE HOUSE®

breakfast & brunch

PECAN WAFFLES

MAKES 8 WAFFLES

2¼ cups all-purpose flour

3 tablespoons sugar

1 tablespoon baking powder

½ teaspoon salt

2 cups milk

2 eggs, beaten

¼ cup vegetable oil

¾ cup chopped pecans, toasted*

Butter and maple syrup

To toast pecans, cook in medium skillet over medium heat 3 to 4 minutes or until lightly browned, stirring frequently.

1. Preheat classic round waffle iron; grease lightly.

2. Combine flour, sugar, baking powder and salt in large bowl. Whisk milk, eggs and oil in medium bowl until well blended. Add to flour mixture; stir just until blended. Stir in pecans.

3. For each waffle, pour about ½ cup batter into waffle iron. Close lid and bake until steaming stops. Serve with butter and maple syrup.

STRAWBERRY-TOPPED PANCAKES

MAKES 2 SERVINGS (6 LARGE PANCAKES)

1½ cups sliced fresh strawberries

2 tablespoons seedless strawberry jam

1¼ cups all-purpose flour

¼ cup sugar

1 teaspoon baking powder

1 teaspoon baking soda

¼ teaspoon salt

1¼ cups buttermilk

1 egg, lightly beaten

1 to 2 tablespoons vegetable oil

Whipped cream (optional)

1. Combine strawberries and strawberry jam in medium bowl; stir gently to coat. Set aside while preparing pancakes.

2. Combine flour, sugar, baking powder, baking soda and salt in large bowl; mix well. Add buttermilk and egg; whisk until blended.

3. Heat 1 tablespoon oil in large skillet* over medium heat or brush griddle with oil. For each pancake, pour ½ cup of batter into skillet, spreading into 5- to 6-inch circle. Cook 3 to 4 minutes or until bottom is golden brown and small bubbles appear on surface. Turn pancake; cook 2 minutes or until golden brown. Add additional oil to skillet as needed.

4. For each serving, stack three pancakes; top with strawberry mixture. Garnish with whipped cream.

*Since pancakes are large, a skillet may not be able to cook more than one at a time. Keep pancakes warm in 250°F oven on wire rack set over baking sheet.

PUMPKIN BREAD

MAKES 2 LOAVES

2¼ cups all-purpose flour

1 tablespoon pumpkin pie spice

1 teaspoon baking powder

1 teaspoon baking soda

¾ teaspoon salt

3 eggs

1 can (15 ounces) pure pumpkin

1 cup granulated sugar

1 cup packed brown sugar

⅔ cup vegetable oil

1 teaspoon vanilla

¼ cup roasted salted pumpkin seeds, coarsely chopped or crushed

1. Preheat oven to 350°F. Spray two 8×4-inch loaf pans with nonstick cooking spray.

2. Combine flour, pumpkin pie spice, baking powder, baking soda and salt in medium bowl; mix well.

3. Beat eggs in large bowl. Add pumpkin, granulated sugar, brown sugar, oil and vanilla; whisk until well blended. Add flour mixture; stir just until dry ingredients are moistened. Divide batter between prepared pans; smooth top. Sprinkle with pumpkin seeds; pat seeds gently into batter to adhere.

4. Bake about 50 minutes or until toothpick inserted into centers comes out mostly clean with just a few moist crumbs. Cool in pans 10 minutes; remove to wire racks to cool completely.

//

note

The recipe can be made in one 9×5-inch loaf pan instead of two 8×4-inch pans. Bake about 1 hour 20 minutes or until toothpick inserted into center comes out with just a few moist crumbs. Check bread after 50 minutes; cover loosely with foil if top is browning too quickly.

appetizers

CHICKEN BACON QUESADILLAS

MAKES 4 SERVINGS

4 teaspoons vegetable oil, divided

4 (8-inch) flour tortillas

1 cup (4 ounces) shredded Colby-Jack cheese

2 cups coarsely chopped cooked chicken

4 slices bacon, crisp-cooked and coarsely chopped

½ cup pico de gallo, plus additional for serving

Sour cream and guacamole (optional)

1. Heat large nonstick skillet over medium heat; brush with 1 teaspoon oil. Place one tortilla in skillet; sprinkle with ¼ cup cheese. Spread ½ cup chicken over one half of tortilla; top with one fourth of bacon and 2 tablespoons pico de gallo.

2. Cook 1 to 2 minutes or until cheese is melted and bottom of tortilla is lightly browned. Fold tortilla over filling, pressing with spatula. Transfer to cutting board; cool slightly. Cut into wedges. Repeat with remaining ingredients. Serve with additional pico de gallo, sour cream and guacamole, if desired.

MOZZARELLA STICKS

MAKES 4 TO 6 SERVINGS

¼ cup all-purpose flour

2 eggs

1 tablespoon water

1 cup plain dry bread
  crumbs

2 teaspoons Italian
  seasoning

½ teaspoon salt

½ teaspoon garlic powder

1 package (12 ounces) string
  cheese (12 sticks)

  Vegetable oil for frying

1 cup marinara or pizza
  sauce, heated

1. Place flour in shallow bowl. Whisk eggs and water in another shallow bowl. Combine bread crumbs, Italian seasoning, salt and garlic powder in third shallow bowl.

2. Coat each piece of cheese with flour. Dip in egg mixture, letting excess drip back into bowl. Roll in bread crumb mixture to coat. Dip again in egg mixture and roll again in bread crumb mixture. Place on plate; refrigerate until ready to cook.

3. Heat 2 inches of oil in large saucepan over medium-high heat to 350°F; adjust heat to maintain temperature. Add cheese sticks; cook about 1 minute or until golden brown. Drain on wire rack. Serve with warm marinara sauce for dipping.

BUFFALO WINGS

MAKES 4 SERVINGS

1 cup hot pepper sauce

⅓ cup vegetable oil, plus additional for frying

1 teaspoon sugar

½ teaspoon ground red pepper

½ teaspoon garlic powder

½ teaspoon Worcestershire sauce

⅛ teaspoon black pepper

1 pound chicken wings, tips discarded, separated at joints

Blue cheese or ranch dressing

Celery sticks

1. Combine hot pepper sauce, ⅓ cup oil, sugar, red pepper, garlic powder, Worcestershire sauce and black pepper in small saucepan; cook over medium heat 20 minutes. Pour sauce into large bowl.

2. Heat 3 inches of oil in large saucepan over medium-high heat to 350°F; adjust heat to maintain temperature during frying. Add wings; cook 10 minutes or until crispy. Drain on wire rack set over paper towels.

3. Transfer wings to bowl of sauce; toss to coat. Serve with blue cheese dressing and celery sticks.

SPINACH-ARTICHOKE DIP

MAKES 6 TO 8 SERVINGS

- 1 package (8 to 10 ounces) baby spinach
- 1 package (8 ounces) cream cheese, softened
- ¼ cup mayonnaise
- 1 clove garlic, minced
- 1 teaspoon dried basil
- ½ teaspoon dried thyme
- ¼ teaspoon salt
- ¼ teaspoon red pepper flakes
- ¼ teaspoon black pepper
- 1 can (about 14 ounces) artichoke hearts, drained and chopped
- ¾ cup grated Parmesan cheese, divided
  Toasted French bread slices or tortilla chips

1. Preheat oven to 350°F. Spray 8-inch oval, round or square baking dish with nonstick cooking spray.

2. Place spinach in large microwavable bowl; cover and microwave on HIGH 2 minutes or until wilted. Uncover; let stand until cool enough to handle. Squeeze dry and coarsely chop.

3. Whisk cream cheese, mayonnaise, garlic, basil, thyme, salt, red pepper flakes and black pepper in medium bowl until well blended. Stir in spinach, artichokes and ½ cup Parmesan. Spread in prepared baking dish; sprinkle with remaining ¼ cup Parmesan.

4. Bake about 30 minutes or until edges are golden brown. Cool slightly; serve warm with toasted bread slices.

THE BIG ONION

MAKES 4 TO 6 SERVINGS

DIPPING SAUCE

- ½ cup mayonnaise
- 2 tablespoons horseradish
- 1 tablespoon ketchup
- ¼ teaspoon paprika
- ⅛ teaspoon salt
- ⅛ teaspoon ground red pepper
- ⅛ teaspoon dried oregano

ONION

- 1 large sweet onion (about 1 pound)
  Ice water
- 1 cup milk
- 2 eggs
- 1½ cups all-purpose flour
- 1 tablespoon paprika
- 1½ teaspoons salt
- 1½ teaspoons ground red pepper
- ¾ teaspoon black pepper
- ½ teaspoon onion powder
- ½ teaspoon garlic powder
- ¼ teaspoon ground cumin
  Vegetable oil for frying

1. For sauce, combine mayonnaise, horseradish, ketchup, ¼ teaspoon paprika, ⅛ teaspoon salt, ⅛ teaspoon red pepper and oregano in small bowl; mix well. Cover and refrigerate until ready to serve.

2. Cut about ½ inch off top of onion and peel off papery skin. Place onion cut side down on cutting board. Starting ½ inch from root, use large sharp knife to make one slice down to cutting board. Repeat slicing all the way around onion to make 12 to 16 evenly spaced cuts. Turn onion over; gently separate outer pieces. Place onion in large bowl of ice water; let soak 15 minutes.

3. Meanwhile, whisk milk and eggs in large bowl. Combine flour, 1 tablespoon paprika, 1½ teaspoons salt, 1½ teaspoons red pepper, black pepper, onion powder, garlic powder and cumin in separate large bowl.

4. Drain onion, place in bowl of flour mixture. Cover onion with flour mixture, making sure it gets between slices and coats onion completely. Dip onion in milk mixture, turning to coat. Let excess milk mixture drip back into bowl before returning onion to flour mixture, turning to make sure all sides of onion and space between slices are well coated. Place onion on plate or baking sheet; refrigerate while heating oil.

5. Pour enough oil into large deep saucepan, Dutch oven or deep fryer to completely cover onion. Heat oil over medium heat to 350°F. Use wire skimmer or large slotted spoon to carefully lower onion into oil, cut sides down. Cook 3 to 4 minutes or until onion is beginning to brown. Turn and cook 3 minutes or until golden brown. Drain on paper towel-lined plate; sprinkle with salt. Serve immediately with dipping sauce.

TEX-MEX NACHOS

MAKES 4 TO 6 SERVINGS

- 1 tablespoon vegetable oil
- 8 ounces ground beef
- ½ cup chopped onion
- 2 cloves garlic, minced
- 2 teaspoons chili powder
- 1 teaspoon ground cumin
- ½ teaspoon salt
- ½ teaspoon dried oregano
- 1 can (about 15 ounces) kidney beans, rinsed and drained
- ½ cup corn
- ½ cup sour cream, divided
- 2 tablespoons mayonnaise
- 1 tablespoon lime juice
- ¼ to ½ teaspoon chipotle chili powder
- ½ bag tortilla chips
- ½ (15-ounce) jar Cheddar cheese dip, warmed
- ½ cup pico de gallo
- ¼ cup guacamole
- 1 cup shredded iceberg lettuce
- 2 jalapeño peppers,* thinly sliced into rings

Jalapeño peppers can sting and irritate the skin, so wear rubber gloves when handling peppers and do not touch your eyes.

1. Heat oil in large skillet over medium-high heat. Add beef, onion and garlic; cook and stir 6 to 8 minutes or until beef is no longer pink. Add chili powder, cumin, salt and oregano; cook and stir 1 minute. Add beans and corn; reduce heat to medium-low and cook 3 minutes or until heated through.

2. Combine ¼ cup sour cream, mayonnaise, lime juice and chipotle chili powder in small bowl; mix well. Pour chipotle sauce into small plastic squeeze bottle.

3. Spread tortilla chips on platter or large plate. Top with beef mixture; drizzle with cheese dip. Top with pico de gallo, guacamole, remaining ¼ cup sour cream, lettuce and jalapeños. Squeeze chipotle sauce over nachos. Serve immediately.

POTATO SKINS

MAKES 6 TO 8 SERVINGS

8 medium baking potatoes (6 to 8 ounces each), unpeeled

1 tablespoon vegetable oil

1 teaspoon salt

⅛ teaspoon black pepper

1 tablespoon butter, melted

1 cup (4 ounces) shredded Cheddar cheese

8 slices bacon, crisp-cooked and coarsely chopped

1 cup sour cream

3 tablespoons snipped fresh chives

1. Preheat oven to 400°F.

2. Prick potatoes all over with fork. Rub oil over potatoes; sprinkle with salt and pepper. Place in 13×9-inch baking pan. Bake 1 hour or until fork-tender. Let stand until cool enough to handle. *Reduce oven temperature to 350°F.*

3. Cut potatoes in half lengthwise; cut small slice off bottom of each half so potato halves lay flat. Scoop out soft middles of potato skins; reserve for another use. Place potato halves, skin sides up, in baking pan; brush potato skins with butter.

4. Bake 20 to 25 minutes or until crisp. Turn potatoes over; top with cheese and bacon. Bake 5 minutes or until cheese is melted. Cool slightly. Top with sour cream and chives just before serving.

CHICKEN PARMESAN SLIDERS

MAKES 12 SLIDERS

- 4 boneless skinless chicken breasts (6 to 8 ounces each)
- ¼ cup all-purpose flour
- 2 eggs
- 1 tablespoon water
- 1 cup Italian-seasoned dry bread crumbs
- ½ cup grated Parmesan cheese
- Salt and black pepper
- Olive oil
- 12 slider buns (about 3 inches), split
- ¾ cup marinara sauce
- 6 tablespoons Alfredo sauce
- 6 slices mozzarella cheese, cut into halves
- 2 tablespoons butter, melted
- ¼ teaspoon garlic powder
- 6 tablespoons pesto sauce

1. Preheat oven to 375°F. Line baking sheet with foil; top with wire rack.

2. Pound chicken to ½-inch thickness between two sheets of plastic wrap with rolling pin or meat mallet. Cut each chicken breast crosswise into three pieces about the size of slider buns.

3. Place flour in shallow dish. Beat eggs and water in second shallow dish. Combine bread crumbs and Parmesan in third shallow dish. Season flour and egg mixtures with pinch of salt and pepper. Coat chicken pieces lightly with flour, shaking off excess. Dip in egg mixture, coating completely; roll in bread crumb mixture to coat. Place on large plate; let stand 10 minutes.

4. Heat ¼ inch oil in large nonstick skillet over medium-high heat. Add chicken in single layer (cook in two batches if necessary); cook 3 to 4 minutes per side or until golden brown. Remove chicken to wire rack; bake 5 minutes or until cooked through (165°F). Remove rack with chicken from baking sheet.

5. Arrange slider buns on foil-lined baking sheet with bottoms cut sides up and tops cut sides down. Spread 1 tablespoon marinara sauce over each bottom bun; top with piece of chicken. Spread ½ tablespoon Alfredo sauce over chicken; top with half slice of mozzarella. Combine butter and garlic powder in small bowl; brush mixture over top buns.

6. Bake 3 to 4 minutes or until mozzarella is melted and top buns are lightly toasted. Spread ½ tablespoon pesto over mozzarella; cover with top buns.

TOASTED RAVIOLI

MAKES 20 TO 24 RAVIOLI

1 cup all-purpose flour

2 eggs

¼ cup water

1 cup plain dry bread
   crumbs

1 teaspoon Italian seasoning

¾ teaspoon garlic powder

¼ teaspoon salt

½ cup grated Parmesan
   cheese

2 tablespoons finely
   chopped fresh parsley

  Vegetable oil for frying

1 package (12 to 16 ounces)
   meat or cheese ravioli,
   thawed if frozen

  Pasta sauce, heated

1. Place flour in shallow bowl. Whisk eggs and water in another shallow bowl. Combine bread crumbs, Italian seasoning, garlic powder and salt in third shallow bowl. Combine cheese and parsley in large bowl; stir to blend.

2. Heat 2 inches of oil in large deep skillet over medium-high heat to 350°F; adjust heat to maintain temperature.

3. Coat ravioli with flour. Dip in egg mixture, letting excess drip back into bowl. Roll in bread crumb mixture to coat.

4. Working in batches, carefully add ravioli to hot oil; cook 1 minute or until golden brown, turning once. Remove from oil with slotted spoon; drain on paper towel-lined plate. Add to bowl with cheese mixture; toss to coat. Serve with warm pasta sauce.

GUACAMOLE

MAKES 2 CUPS

2 large ripe avocados

2 teaspoons fresh lime juice

¼ cup finely chopped red onion

2 tablespoons chopped fresh cilantro

½ jalapeño pepper,* finely chopped

½ teaspoon salt

*Jalapeño peppers can sting and irritate the skin, so wear rubber gloves when handling peppers and do not touch your eyes.

1. Cut avocados in half lengthwise around pits. Remove pits. Scoop avocados into large bowl; sprinkle with lime juice and toss to coat. Mash to desired consistency with fork or potato masher.

2. Add onion, cilantro, jalapeño and salt; stir gently until well blended. Taste and add additional salt, if desired.

ZUCCHINI FRITTE

MAKES 4 SERVINGS

Lemon Aioli
(recipe follows)

Vegetable oil for frying

¾ to 1 cup soda water

½ cup all-purpose flour

¼ cup cornstarch

½ teaspoon coarse salt

¼ teaspoon garlic powder

¼ teaspoon dried oregano

¼ teaspoon black pepper

3 cups panko bread crumbs

1½ pounds medium zucchini
(6 to 8 inches long),
ends trimmed, cut
lengthwise into
¼-inch-thick slices

¼ cup grated Parmesan
or Romano cheese

Chopped fresh parsley

Lemon wedges

1. Prepare Lemon Aioli; cover and refrigerate until ready to use.

2. Line baking sheet with paper towels; set aside. Pour oil into large saucepan or Dutch oven to depth of 2 inches; heat to 350°F over medium-high heat.

3. Meanwhile, pour ¾ cup soda water into large bowl. Combine flour, cornstarch, salt, garlic powder, oregano and pepper in small bowl; mix well. Slowly whisk flour mixture into soda water just until blended. Add additional soda water if necessary to reach consistency of thin pancake batter. Place panko in medium bowl.

4. Working with one at a time, dip zucchini slices into batter to coat; let excess batter drip back into bowl. Add to bowl with panko; press panko into zucchini slices to coat both sides completely. Place zucchini on prepared baking sheet.

5. Fry zucchini slices in batches 3 to 4 minutes or until golden brown. (Return oil to 350°F between batches.) Drain on paper towel-lined plate. Sprinkle with cheese and parsley; serve with Lemon Aioli and lemon wedges.

//

lemon aioli

Combine ½ cup mayonnaise, 2 tablespoons lemon juice, 1 tablespoon chopped fresh Italian parsley and 1 teaspoon minced garlic in small bowl; mix well. Season with salt and pepper.

BUFFALO CHICKEN DIP

MAKES 5 CUPS

- 2 packages (8 ounces each) cream cheese, softened and cut into pieces
- 1 jar (12 ounces) restaurant-style wing sauce
- 1 cup ranch dressing
- 2 cups shredded cooked chicken (from 1 pound boneless skinless chicken breasts)
- 2 cups (8 ounces) shredded Cheddar cheese
  Tortilla chips
  Celery sticks

1. Combine cream cheese, wing sauce and ranch dressing in large saucepan; cook over medium-low heat 7 to 10 minutes or until cream cheese is melted and mixture is smooth, whisking frequently.

2. Combine chicken and Cheddar cheese in large bowl. Add cream cheese mixture; stir until well blended. Pour into serving bowl; serve warm with tortilla chips and celery sticks.

BRUSCHETTA

MAKES 8 SERVINGS (1 CUP)

- 4 plum tomatoes, seeded and diced
- ½ cup packed fresh basil leaves, finely chopped
- 5 tablespoons olive oil, divided
- 2 cloves garlic, minced
- 2 teaspoons finely chopped oil-packed sun-dried tomatoes
- ¼ teaspoon salt
- ⅛ teaspoon black pepper
- 16 slices Italian bread
- 2 tablespoons grated Parmesan cheese

1. Combine fresh tomatoes, basil, 3 tablespoons oil, garlic, sun-dried tomatoes, salt and pepper in large bowl; mix well. Let stand at room temperature 1 hour to blend flavors.

2. Preheat oven to 375°F. Place bread on baking sheet. Brush remaining 2 tablespoons oil over one side of bread slices; sprinkle with cheese. Bake 6 to 8 minutes or until toasted.

3. Top each bread slice with 1 tablespoon tomato mixture.

WHITE SPINACH QUESO

MAKES 4 TO 6 SERVINGS

1 tablespoon olive oil

1 clove garlic, minced

1 tablespoon all-purpose flour

1 can (12 ounces) evaporated milk

½ teaspoon salt

2 cups (8 ounces) shredded Monterey Jack cheese, divided

1 package (10 ounces) frozen chopped spinach, thawed and squeezed dry

Optional toppings: pico de gallo, guacamole, chopped fresh cilantro and queso fresco

Tortilla chips

1. Preheat broiler.

2. Heat oil in medium saucepan over medium-low heat. Add garlic; cook and stir 1 minute without browning. Add flour; whisk until smooth. Add evaporated milk in thin, steady stream, whisking constantly. Stir in salt. Cook about 4 minutes or until slightly thickened, whisking frequently.

3. Add 1½ cups Monterey Jack cheese; whisk until smooth. Stir in spinach. Pour into medium cast iron skillet; sprinkle with remaining ½ cup Monterey Jack cheese.

4. Broil 1 minute or until cheese is melted and browned in spots. Top with pico de gallo, guacamole, cilantro and queso fresco. Serve immediately with tortilla chips.

ONION RING STACK

MAKES 4 TO 6 SERVINGS (ABOUT 20 ONION RINGS)

1 cup all-purpose flour,
   divided

½ cup cornmeal

1 teaspoon black pepper

½ teaspoon salt, plus
   additional for seasoning

¼ to ½ teaspoon ground
   red pepper

1 cup light-colored beer

Rémoulade Sauce
   (recipe follows) or
   ranch dressing

Vegetable oil for frying

6 tablespoons cornstarch,
   divided

2 large sweet onions, cut
   into ½-inch rings and
   separated

1. Combine ½ cup flour, cornmeal, black pepper, ½ teaspoon salt and red pepper in large bowl; mix well. Whisk in beer until well blended. Let batter stand 1 hour.

2. Prepare Rémoulade Sauce; refrigerate until ready to serve.

3. Pour oil into large saucepan or Dutch oven to depth of 2 inches; heat to 360° to 370°F. Line large wire rack with paper towels.

4. Whisk 4 tablespoons cornstarch into batter. Combine remaining ½ cup flour and 2 tablespoons cornstarch in medium bowl. Thoroughly coat onions with flour mixture.

5. Working with one at a time, dip onion rings into batter to coat completely; carefully place in hot oil. Cook about 4 onions rings at a time 3 minutes or until golden brown, turning once. Remove to prepared wire rack; season with additional salt. Return oil to 370°F between batches. Serve immediately with Rémoulade Sauce.

/ /

rémoulade sauce

Combine 1 cup mayonnaise, 2 tablespoons coarse-grain mustard, 1 tablespoon lemon juice, 1 tablespoon sweet relish, 1 teaspoon horseradish sauce, 1 teaspoon Worcestershire sauce and ¼ teaspoon hot pepper sauce in medium bowl; mix well.

SALSA

MAKES 4½ CUPS

- 1 can (28 ounces) whole Italian plum tomatoes, undrained
- 2 fresh plum tomatoes, seeded and coarsely chopped
- 2 tablespoons canned diced mild green chiles
- 1 tablespoon canned diced jalapeño peppers* (optional)
- 1 tablespoon white vinegar
- 1 clove garlic, minced
- 1 teaspoon onion powder
- 1 teaspoon sugar
- 1 teaspoon ground cumin
- ½ teaspoon garlic powder
- ¼ teaspoon salt

  Tortilla chips

  Jalapeño peppers can sting and irritate the skin, so wear rubber gloves when handling peppers and do not touch your eyes.

Combine tomatoes with juice, fresh tomatoes, green chiles, jalapeños, if desired, vinegar, garlic, onion powder, sugar, cumin, garlic powder and salt in food processor; process until finely chopped. Serve with tortilla chips.

PEPPERONI STUFFED MUSHROOMS

MAKES 4 TO 6 SERVINGS

16 medium mushrooms

1 tablespoon olive oil

½ cup finely chopped onion

2 ounces pepperoni, finely chopped (about ½ cup)

¼ cup finely chopped green bell pepper

½ teaspoon seasoned salt

¼ teaspoon dried oregano

⅛ teaspoon black pepper

½ cup crushed buttery crackers (about 12)

¼ cup grated Parmesan cheese

1 tablespoon chopped fresh parsley, plus additional for garnish

1. Preheat oven to 350°F. Line baking sheet with foil; spray foil with nonstick cooking spray.

2. Clean mushrooms; remove stems and set aside caps. Finely chop stems.

3. Heat oil in large skillet over medium-high heat. Add onion; cook and stir 2 to 3 minutes or until softened. Add mushroom stems, pepperoni, bell pepper, seasoned salt, oregano and black pepper; cook and stir about 5 minutes or until vegetables are tender but not browned.

4. Remove from heat; stir in crushed crackers, cheese and 1 tablespoon parsley until blended. Spoon mixture into mushroom caps, mounding slightly in centers. Place filled caps on prepared baking sheet.

5. Bake about 20 minutes or until heated through. Garnish with additional parsley.

CRAB SHACK DIP

MAKES 6 TO 8 SERVINGS (ABOUT 3½ CUPS)

- ½ (8-ounce) package cream cheese, softened
- ½ cup sour cream
- 2 tablespoons mayonnaise
- ¾ teaspoon seasoned salt
- ¼ teaspoon paprika, plus additional for garnish
- 2 cans (6 ounces each) crabmeat, drained and flaked
- ½ cup (2 ounces) shredded mozzarella cheese
- 2 tablespoons minced onion
- 2 tablespoons finely chopped green bell pepper*
- Chopped fresh parsley (optional)
- Tortilla chips

For a spicier dip, substitute 1 tablespoon minced jalapeño pepper for the bell pepper.

1. Preheat oven to 350°F.

2. Combine cream cheese, sour cream, mayonnaise, seasoned salt and ¼ teaspoon paprika in medium bowl; stir until well blended and smooth. Add crabmeat, cheese, onion and bell pepper; stir until blended. Spread in small (1-quart) shallow baking dish.

3. Bake 15 to 20 minutes or until bubbly and top is beginning to brown. Garnish with additional paprika and parsley; serve with tortilla chips.

CHICKEN LETTUCE WRAPS

MAKES 6 TO 8 SERVINGS

- 1 tablespoon vegetable oil
- 1 small onion, finely chopped
- 5 ounces cremini mushrooms, finely chopped (about 2 cups)
- 1 pound ground chicken
- ¼ cup hoisin sauce
- 2 tablespoons soy sauce
- 1 tablespoon rice vinegar
- 1 tablespoon sriracha sauce
- 1 tablespoon oyster sauce
- 2 cloves garlic, minced
- 1 teaspoon grated fresh ginger
- 1 teaspoon dark sesame oil
- ½ cup finely chopped water chestnuts
- 2 green onions, thinly sliced
- 1 head butter lettuce

1. Heat vegetable oil in large skillet over medium-high heat. Add onion; cook and stir 2 minutes. Add mushrooms; cook about 8 minutes or until lightly browned and liquid has evaporated, stirring occasionally.

2. Add chicken; cook about 8 minutes or until no longer pink, stirring to break up meat. Stir in hoisin sauce, soy sauce, vinegar, sriracha, oyster sauce, garlic, ginger and sesame oil; cook 4 minutes. Add water chestnuts; cook and stir 2 minutes or until heated through. Remove from heat; stir in green onions.

3. Separate lettuce leaves. Spoon about ¼ cup chicken mixture into each lettuce leaf. Serve immediately.

SPINACH FLORENTINE FLATBREAD

MAKES 8 SERVINGS

- 1 tablespoon olive oil
- 2 cloves garlic, minced
- 1 package (8 to 10 ounces) baby spinach
- 1 can (about 14 ounces) quartered artichoke hearts, drained and sliced
- ½ teaspoon salt
- ¼ teaspoon dried oregano
  Pinch black pepper
  Pinch red pepper flakes
- 2 rectangular pizza or flatbread crusts (about 8 ounces each)
- 1 plum tomato, seeded and diced
- 2 cups (8 ounces) shredded Monterey Jack cheese
- ½ cup (2 ounces) shredded Italian cheese blend
  Shredded fresh basil leaves (optional)

1. Preheat oven to 425°F.

2. Heat oil in large skillet over medium-high heat. Add garlic; cook and stir 30 seconds. Add half of spinach; cook and stir until slightly wilted. Add additional spinach by handfuls; cook about 3 minutes or until completely wilted, stirring occasionally. Transfer to medium bowl; stir in artichokes, salt and oregano. Season with black pepper and red pepper flakes.

3. Place pizza crusts on large baking sheet. Spread spinach mixture over crusts; sprinkle with tomato, Monterey Jack cheese and Italian cheese blend.

4. Bake 12 minutes or until cheeses are melted and edges of crusts are browned. Garnish with basil.

////////////////////////////////////

tip

For crispier crusts, bake flatbreads on a preheated pizza stone or directly on the oven rack.

soups

INSPIRED BY
PANERA BREAD®

BROCCOLI CHEESE SOUP

MAKES 4 TO 6 SERVINGS

6 tablespoons (¾ stick) butter

1 cup chopped onion

1 clove garlic, minced

¼ cup all-purpose flour

2 cups vegetable broth

2 cups milk

1½ teaspoons Dijon mustard

½ teaspoon salt

¼ teaspoon ground nutmeg

¼ teaspoon black pepper

⅛ teaspoon hot pepper sauce

1 package (16 ounces) frozen broccoli (5 cups)

2 carrots, shredded (1 cup)

6 ounces pasteurized process cheese product, cubed

1 cup (4 ounces) shredded sharp Cheddar cheese, plus additional for garnish

1. Melt butter in large saucepan or Dutch oven over medium-low heat. Add onion; cook and stir 8 minutes or until softened. Add garlic; cook and stir 1 minute. Increase heat to medium. Whisk in flour until smooth; cook and stir 3 minutes without browning.

2. Gradually whisk in broth and milk. Add mustard, salt, nutmeg, black pepper and hot pepper sauce; cook 15 minutes or until thickened, stirring occasionally.

3. Add broccoli; cook 15 minutes. Add carrots; cook 10 minutes or until vegetables are tender.

4. Transfer half of soup to food processor or blender; process until smooth. Return to saucepan. Add cheese product and 1 cup Cheddar; cook and stir over low heat until cheese is melted. Garnish soup with additional Cheddar.

BLACK BEAN SOUP

MAKES 4 TO 6 SERVINGS

- 2 tablespoons vegetable oil
- 1 cup diced onion
- 1 stalk celery, diced
- 2 carrots, diced
- ½ small green bell pepper, diced
- 4 cloves garlic, minced
- 4 cans (about 15 ounces each) black beans, rinsed and drained, divided
- 4 cups (32 ounces) chicken or vegetable broth, divided
- 2 tablespoons cider vinegar
- 2 teaspoons chili powder
- ½ teaspoon salt
- ½ teaspoon ground red pepper
- ½ teaspoon ground cumin
- ¼ teaspoon liquid smoke

  Optional toppings: sour cream, chopped green onions and shredded Cheddar cheese

1. Heat oil in large saucepan or Dutch oven over medium-low heat. Add onion, celery, carrots, bell pepper and garlic; cook 10 minutes, stirring occasionally.

2. Combine half of beans and 1 cup broth in food processor or blender; process until smooth. Add to vegetables in saucepan.

3. Stir in remaining beans, 3 cups broth, vinegar, chili powder, salt, red pepper, cumin and liquid smoke; bring to a boil over high heat. Reduce heat to medium-low; cook 1 hour or until vegetables are tender and soup is thickened, stirring occasionally. Garnish as desired.

HEARTY TUSCAN SOUP

MAKES 6 TO 8 SERVINGS

1 teaspoon olive oil

1 pound bulk mild or hot Italian sausage*

1 medium onion, chopped

3 cloves garlic, minced

¼ cup all-purpose flour

5 cups chicken broth

1 teaspoon salt

½ teaspoon Italian seasoning

3 medium unpeeled russet potatoes (about 1 pound), halved lengthwise and thinly sliced

2 cups packed torn stemmed kale leaves

1 cup half-and-half or whipping cream

Or use sausage links and remove from casings.

1. Heat oil in large saucepan or Dutch oven over medium-high heat. Add sausage; cook until sausage begins to brown, stirring to break up meat. Add onion and garlic; cook about 5 minutes or until onion is softened and sausage is browned, stirring occasionally.

2. Stir in flour until blended. Add broth, salt and Italian seasoning; bring to a boil. Stir in potatoes and kale. Reduce heat to medium-low; cook 15 to 20 minutes or until potatoes are fork-tender.

3. Reduce heat to low; stir in half-and-half. Cook about 5 minutes or until heated through.

CHICKEN ENCHILADA SOUP

MAKES 8 TO 10 SERVINGS

2 tablespoons vegetable oil, divided

1½ pounds boneless skinless chicken breasts, cut into ½-inch pieces

½ cup chopped onion

2 cloves garlic, minced

2 cans (about 14 ounces each) chicken broth

3 cups water, divided

1 cup masa harina

1 package (16 ounces) pasteurized process cheese product, cubed

1 can (10 ounces) mild red enchilada sauce

1 teaspoon chili powder

½ teaspoon salt

½ teaspoon ground cumin

1 large tomato, seeded and chopped

Crispy tortilla strips*

If tortilla strips are not available, crumble tortilla chips into bite-size pieces.

1. Heat 1 tablespoon oil in large saucepan or Dutch oven over medium-high heat. Add chicken; cook and stir 10 minutes or until no longer pink. Transfer to medium bowl with slotted spoon; drain excess liquid from saucepan.

2. Heat remaining 1 tablespoon oil in same saucepan over medium-high heat. Add onion and garlic; cook and stir 3 minutes or until softened. Stir in broth.

3. Whisk 2 cups water into masa harina in large bowl until smooth. Whisk mixture into broth in saucepan. Stir in remaining 1 cup water, cheese product, enchilada sauce, chili powder, salt and cumin; bring to a boil over high heat. Add chicken. Reduce heat to medium-low; cook 30 minutes, stirring frequently. Serve soup with tomato and tortilla strips.

BAKED POTATO SOUP

MAKES 6 TO 8 SERVINGS

- 3 medium russet potatoes (about 1 pound)
- ¼ cup (½ stick) butter
- 1 cup chopped onion
- ½ cup all-purpose flour
- 4 cups chicken or vegetable broth
- 1½ cups instant mashed potato flakes
- 1 cup water
- 1 cup half-and-half
- 1 teaspoon salt
- ½ teaspoon dried basil
- ½ teaspoon dried thyme
- ¼ teaspoon black pepper
- 1 cup (4 ounces) shredded Cheddar cheese
- 4 slices bacon, crisp-cooked and crumbled
- 1 green onion, chopped

1. Preheat oven to 400°F. Scrub potatoes and prick in several places with fork. Place in baking pan; bake 1 hour. Cool completely; peel and cut into ½-inch cubes. (Potatoes can be prepared several days in advance; refrigerate until ready to use.)

2. Melt butter in large saucepan or Dutch oven over medium heat. Add onion; cook and stir 3 minutes or until softened. Whisk in flour; cook and stir 1 minute. Gradually whisk in broth until well blended. Stir in mashed potato flakes, water, half-and-half, salt, basil, thyme and pepper; bring to a boil over medium-high heat. Reduce heat to medium; cook 5 minutes.

3. Stir in baked potato cubes; cook 10 to 15 minutes or until soup is thickened and heated through. Ladle into bowls; top with cheese, bacon and green onion.

BEEF VEGETABLE SOUP

MAKES 6 TO 8 SERVINGS

1½ pounds cubed beef
      stew meat

¼ cup all-purpose flour

3 tablespoons vegetable oil,
      divided

1 onion, chopped

2 stalks celery, chopped

3 tablespoons tomato paste

2 teaspoons salt

1 teaspoon dried thyme

½ teaspoon garlic powder

¼ teaspoon black pepper

6 cups beef broth, divided

1 can (28 ounces) stewed
      tomatoes, undrained

1 tablespoon Worcestershire
      sauce

1 bay leaf

4 unpeeled red potatoes
      (about 1 pound), cut
      into 1-inch pieces

3 medium carrots, cut in
      half lengthwise and
      cut into ½-inch slices

6 ounces green beans,
      trimmed and cut
      into 1-inch pieces

1 cup frozen corn

1. Combine beef and flour in medium bowl; toss to coat. Heat 1 tablespoon oil in large saucepan or Dutch oven over medium-high heat. Cook beef in two batches 5 minutes or until browned, adding additional 1 tablespoon oil after first batch. Remove beef to medium bowl.

2. Heat remaining 1 tablespoon oil in same saucepan. Add onion and celery; cook and stir 5 minutes or until softened. Add tomato paste, 2 teaspoons salt, thyme, garlic powder and pepper; cook and stir 1 minute. Stir in 1 cup broth, scraping up browned bits from bottom of saucepan. Stir in remaining 5 cups broth, tomatoes with juice, Worcestershire sauce, bay leaf and beef; bring to a boil.

3. Reduce heat to low; cover and cook 1 hour and 20 minutes. Add potatoes and carrots; cook 15 minutes. Add green beans and corn; cook 15 minutes or until vegetables are tender. Remove and discard bay leaf. Season with additional salt and pepper.

MINESTRONE SOUP

MAKES 4 TO 6 SERVINGS

1 tablespoon olive oil

½ cup chopped onion

1 stalk celery, diced

1 carrot, diced

2 cloves garlic, minced

2 cups vegetable broth

1½ cups water

1 bay leaf

¾ teaspoon salt

½ teaspoon dried basil

½ teaspoon dried oregano

¼ teaspoon dried thyme

¼ teaspoon sugar

Ground black pepper

1 can (about 15 ounces) dark red kidney beans, rinsed and drained

1 can (about 15 ounces) navy beans or cannellini beans, rinsed and drained

1 can (about 14 ounces) diced tomatoes

1 cup diced zucchini (about 1 small)

½ cup uncooked small shell pasta

½ cup frozen cut green beans

¼ cup dry red wine

1 cup packed chopped fresh spinach

Grated Parmesan cheese (optional)

1. Heat oil in large saucepan or Dutch oven over medium-high heat. Add onion, celery, carrot and garlic; cook and stir 5 to 7 minutes or until vegetables are tender. Add broth, water, bay leaf, salt, basil, oregano, thyme, sugar and pepper; bring to a boil.

2. Stir in kidney beans, navy beans, tomatoes, zucchini, pasta, green beans and wine; cook 10 minutes, stirring occasionally.

3. Add spinach; cook 2 minutes or until pasta and zucchini are tender. Remove and discard bay leaf. Serve with cheese, if desired.

CLASSIC FRENCH ONION SOUP

MAKES 4 SERVINGS

3 tablespoons butter

3 large yellow onions (about 2 pounds), sliced

3 cans (about 14 ounces each) beef broth

½ cup dry sherry

½ teaspoon salt

½ teaspoon dried thyme

½ teaspoon white pepper

4 slices French bread, toasted

1 cup (4 ounces) shredded Swiss cheese

1. Melt butter in large saucepan or Dutch oven over medium-high heat. Add onions, cook 15 minutes or until lightly browned, stirring occasionally. Reduce heat to medium; cook 30 to 40 minutes or until onions are deep golden brown, stirring occasionally.

2. Stir in broth, sherry, salt, thyme and pepper; bring to a boil. Reduce heat to low; cook 20 minutes. Preheat broiler.

3. Ladle soup into four heatproof bowls; top with bread slices and cheese. Broil 4 inches from heat source 2 to 3 minutes or until cheese is bubbly and browned.

PASTA FAGIOLI

MAKES 8 SERVINGS

2 tablespoons olive oil, divided

1 pound ground beef

1 cup chopped onion

1 cup diced carrots (about 2 medium)

1 cup diced celery (about 2 stalks)

3 cloves garlic, minced

4 cups beef broth

1 can (28 ounces) diced tomatoes

1 can (15 ounces) tomato sauce

1 tablespoon cider vinegar

2 teaspoons sugar

1½ teaspoons dried basil

1¼ teaspoons salt

1 teaspoon dried oregano

¾ teaspoon dried thyme

2 cups uncooked ditalini pasta

1 can (about 15 ounces) dark red kidney beans, rinsed and drained

1 can (about 15 ounces) cannellini beans, rinsed and drained

Grated Romano cheese

1. Heat 1 tablespoon oil in large saucepan or Dutch oven over medium-high heat. Add beef; cook 5 minutes or until browned, stirring to break up meat. Transfer to medium bowl; set aside. Drain fat.

2. Heat remaining 1 tablespoon oil in same saucepan over medium-high heat. Add onion, carrots and celery; cook and stir 5 minutes or until vegetables are tender. Add garlic; cook and stir 1 minute. Add cooked beef, broth, tomatoes, tomato sauce, vinegar, sugar, basil, salt, oregano and thyme; bring to a boil. Reduce heat to medium-low; cover and cook 30 minutes.

3. Add pasta, kidney beans and cannellini beans; cook over medium heat 10 minutes or until pasta is tender, stirring frequently. Sprinkle with cheese.

HARVEST PUMPKIN SOUP

MAKES 8 SERVINGS

1 sugar pumpkin or acorn
   squash (about 2 pounds)

1 kabocha or butternut
   squash (about 2 pounds)

   Salt and black pepper

2 tablespoons olive oil

2 tablespoons butter

1 large onion, finely
   chopped

2 stalks celery, chopped

1 medium carrot, chopped

¼ cup packed brown sugar

2 tablespoons tomato paste

1 tablespoon minced
   fresh ginger

1 clove garlic, minced

1 teaspoon salt

1 teaspoon ground
   cinnamon

¼ teaspoon ground cumin

¼ teaspoon black pepper

4 cups vegetable broth

1 cup milk

2 teaspoons lemon juice

   Roasted pumpkin seeds
   (optional, see Tip)

1. Preheat oven to 400°F. Line large baking sheet with foil; spray with nonstick cooking spray.

2. Cut pumpkin and kabocha squash in half; remove and discard seeds and strings. Season cut sides with salt and pepper. Place cut sides down on prepared baking sheet; bake 30 to 45 minutes or until fork-tender. When squash is cool enough to handle, remove skin; chop flesh into 1-inch pieces.

3. Heat oil and butter in large saucepan or Dutch oven over medium-high heat. Add onion, celery and carrot; cook and stir 5 minutes or until vegetables are tender. Add brown sugar, tomato paste, ginger, garlic, 1 teaspoon salt, cinnamon, cumin and ¼ teaspoon pepper; cook and stir 1 minute. Stir in broth and squash; bring to a boil. Reduce heat to medium; cook 20 minutes or until squash is very soft.

4. Blend soup with hand-held immersion blender until desired consistency. (Or process in batches in food processor or blender.) Stir in milk and lemon juice; cook until heated through. Garnish with pumpkin seeds.

/////////////////////////////////

tip

Roasted pumpkin seeds can be found at many supermarkets, or you can roast the seeds that you remove from the pumpkin (and the squash) in the recipe. Combine the seeds with 1 teaspoon vegetable oil and ⅛ teaspoon salt in a small bowl; toss to coat. Spread in a single layer on a small foil-lined baking sheet; bake at 300°F 20 to 25 minutes or until the seeds begin to brown, stirring once.

VEGETARIAN CHILI

MAKES 8 TO 10 SERVINGS

2 tablespoons olive oil

1 onion, finely chopped

2 medium carrots, chopped

1 red bell pepper, chopped

3 tablespoons chili powder

2 tablespoons ground cumin

2 tablespoons tomato paste

2 tablespoons packed
   dark brown sugar

3 cloves garlic, minced

1 tablespoon dried oregano

1 teaspoon salt

1 can (28 ounces)
   diced tomatoes

1 can (15 ounces)
   tomato sauce

1 can (about 15 ounces)
   small white beans,
   rinsed and drained

1 can (about 15 ounces)
   light kidney beans,
   rinsed and drained

1 can (about 15 ounces)
   dark kidney beans,
   rinsed and drained

1 can (about 15 ounces)
   pinto beans, rinsed
   and drained

1 cup vegetable broth

1 can (4 ounces) diced
   mild green chiles

1 ounce unsweetened
   baking chocolate,
   chopped

1 tablespoon cider vinegar

1. Heat oil in large saucepan or Dutch oven over medium-high heat. Add onion, carrots and bell pepper; cook 10 minutes or until vegetables are tender, stirring frequently. Add chili powder, cumin, tomato paste, brown sugar, garlic, oregano and salt; cook and stir 1 minute.

2. Stir in tomatoes, tomato sauce, beans, broth, chiles and chocolate; bring to a boil. Reduce heat to medium; cook 20 minutes, stirring occasionally. Stir in vinegar.

PEPPERY SICILIAN CHICKEN SOUP

MAKES 8 TO 10 SERVINGS

2 tablespoons olive oil

1 onion, chopped

1 green bell pepper, chopped

3 stalks celery, chopped

3 carrots, chopped

3 cloves garlic, minced

1 tablespoon salt

3 containers (32 ounces each) chicken broth

2 pounds boneless skinless chicken breasts

1 can (28 ounces) diced tomatoes

2 baking potatoes, peeled and cut into ¼-inch pieces

1½ teaspoons ground white pepper*

1½ teaspoons ground black pepper

½ cup chopped fresh parsley

8 ounces uncooked ditalini pasta

Or substitute additional black pepper for the white pepper.

1. Heat oil in large saucepan or Dutch oven over medium heat. Stir in onion, bell pepper, celery and carrots. Reduce heat to medium-low; cover and cook 10 to 15 minutes or until vegetables are tender but not browned, stirring occasionally. Stir in garlic and 1 tablespoon salt; cover and cook 5 minutes.

2. Stir in broth, chicken, tomatoes, potatoes, white pepper and black pepper; bring to a boil. Reduce heat to low; cover and cook 1 hour. Remove chicken to plate; set aside until cool enough to handle. Shred chicken and return to saucepan with parsley.

3. Meanwhile, cook pasta in medium saucepan of boiling salted water 7 minutes (or 1 minute less than package directs for al dente). Drain pasta and add to soup. Taste and season with additional salt, if desired.

CREAMY TOMATO SOUP

MAKES 6 SERVINGS

soups

- 3 tablespoons olive oil, divided
- 2 tablespoons butter
- 1 large onion, finely chopped
- 2 cloves garlic, minced
- 2 teaspoons sugar
- 1 teaspoon salt
- ½ teaspoon dried oregano
- 2 cans (28 ounces each) peeled Italian plum tomatoes, undrained
- 4 cups ½-inch focaccia cubes (half of 9-ounce loaf)
- ½ teaspoon black pepper
- ½ cup whipping cream

1. Heat 2 tablespoons oil and butter in large saucepan or Dutch oven over medium-high heat. Add onion; cook and stir 5 minutes or until softened. Add garlic, sugar, salt and oregano; cook and stir 30 seconds. Stir in tomatoes with juice; bring to a boil. Reduce heat to medium-low; cook 45 minutes, stirring occasionally.

2. Meanwhile, prepare croutons. Preheat oven to 350°F. Combine focaccia cubes, remaining 1 tablespoon oil and pepper in large bowl; toss to coat. Spread on large rimmed baking sheet. Bake about 10 minutes or until bread cubes are golden brown.

3. Blend soup with hand-held immersion blender until smooth. (Or process soup in batches in food processor or blender.) Stir in cream; cook until heated through. Serve soup topped with croutons.

ITALIAN WEDDING SOUP

MAKES 8 SERVINGS

MEATBALLS

- 2 eggs
- 2 cloves garlic, minced
- 1 teaspoon salt
- ⅛ teaspoon black pepper
- 1½ pounds meat loaf mix (ground beef and pork)
- ¾ cup plain dry bread crumbs
- ½ cup grated Parmesan cheese
- 2 tablespoons olive oil

SOUP

- 1 onion, chopped
- 2 carrots, chopped
- 4 cloves garlic, minced
- 2 heads escarole or curly endive, coarsely chopped
- 8 cups chicken broth
- 1 can (about 14 ounces) Italian plum tomatoes, undrained, coarsely chopped
- 3 sprigs fresh thyme
- 1 teaspoon salt
- ½ teaspoon red pepper flakes
- 1 cup uncooked acini di pepe pasta

1. Whisk eggs, 2 cloves garlic, 1 teaspoon salt and black pepper in large bowl until blended. Stir in meat loaf mix, bread crumbs and cheese; mix gently until well blended. Shape mixture by tablespoonfuls into 1-inch balls.

2. Heat oil in large saucepan or Dutch oven over medium heat. Cook meatballs in batches 5 minutes or until browned. Remove to plate; set aside.

3. Add onion, carrots and 4 cloves garlic to saucepan; cook and stir 5 minutes or until onion is lightly browned. Add escarole; cook 2 minutes or until wilted. Stir in broth, tomatoes with juice, thyme, 1 teaspoon salt and red pepper flakes; bring to a boil over high heat. Reduce heat to medium-low; cook 15 minutes.

4. Add meatballs and pasta to soup; return to a boil over high heat. Reduce heat to medium; cook 10 minutes or until pasta is tender. Remove and discard thyme sprigs before serving.

GARDEN VEGETABLE SOUP

MAKES 8 TO 10 SERVINGS

- 1 tablespoon olive oil
- 1 medium onion, chopped
- 1 carrot, chopped
- 1 stalk celery, chopped
- 1 medium zucchini, diced
- 1 medium yellow squash, diced
- 1 red bell pepper, diced
- 2 tablespoons tomato paste
- 2 cloves garlic, minced
- 2 teaspoons salt
- 1 teaspoon Italian seasoning
- ½ teaspoon black pepper
- 8 cups vegetable broth
- 1 can (28 ounces) whole tomatoes, undrained, coarsely chopped
- ½ cup uncooked pearl barley
- 1 cup cut green beans (1-inch pieces)
- ½ cup corn
- ¼ cup slivered fresh basil
- 1 tablespoon lemon juice

1. Heat oil in large saucepan or Dutch oven over medium-high heat. Add onion, carrot and celery; cook and stir 8 minutes or until vegetables are softened. Add zucchini, yellow squash and bell pepper; cook and stir 5 minutes or until softened.

2. Add tomato paste, garlic, salt, Italian seasoning and black pepper; cook and stir 1 minute. Stir in broth and tomatoes with juice; bring to a boil. Stir in barley. Reduce heat to low; cook 30 minutes.

3. Stir in green beans and corn; cook about 15 minutes or until barley is tender and green beans are crisp-tender. Stir in basil and lemon juice.

LENTIL SOUP

MAKES 6 TO 8 SERVINGS

INSPIRED BY
BERTUCCI'S®
BRICK OVEN PIZZA
& PASTA

- 2 tablespoons olive oil, divided
- 2 medium onions, chopped
- 1½ teaspoons salt
- 4 cloves garlic, minced
- ¼ cup tomato paste
- 1 teaspoon dried oregano
- ½ teaspoon dried basil
- ¼ teaspoon dried thyme
- ¼ teaspoon black pepper
- ½ cup dry sherry or white wine
- 8 cups vegetable broth
- 2 cups water
- 3 carrots, cut into ½-inch pieces
- 2 cups dried lentils, rinsed and sorted
- 1 cup chopped fresh parsley
- 1 tablespoon balsamic vinegar

1. Heat 1 tablespoon oil in large saucepan or Dutch oven over medium heat. Add onions; cook 10 minutes, stirring occasionally. Add remaining 1 tablespoon oil and salt; cook 10 minutes or until onions are golden brown, stirring frequently.

2. Add garlic; cook and stir 1 minute. Add tomato paste, oregano, basil, thyme and pepper; cook and stir 1 minute. Stir in sherry; cook 30 seconds, scraping up browned bits from bottom of saucepan.

3. Stir in broth, water, carrots and lentils; cover and bring to a boil over high heat. Reduce heat to medium-low; cook, partially covered, 30 minutes or until lentils are tender.

4. Remove from heat; stir in parsley and vinegar.

soups

CHICKEN AND GNOCCHI SOUP

MAKES 6 TO 8 SERVINGS

INSPIRED BY
OLIVE GARDEN®
ITALIAN
KITCHEN

- ¼ cup (½ stick) butter
- 1 tablespoon extra virgin olive oil
- 1 cup finely diced onion
- 2 stalks celery, finely chopped
- 2 cloves garlic, minced
- ¼ cup all-purpose flour
- 4 cups half-and-half
- 1 can (about 14 ounces) chicken broth
- 1 teaspoon salt
- ½ teaspoon dried thyme
- ½ teaspoon dried parsley flakes
- ¼ teaspoon ground nutmeg
- 1 package (about 16 ounces) uncooked gnocchi
- 1 package (6 ounces) fully cooked chicken strips, chopped *or* 1 cup diced cooked chicken
- 1 cup shredded carrots
- 1 cup coarsely chopped fresh spinach

1. Melt butter in large saucepan or Dutch oven over medium heat; add oil. Add onion, celery and garlic; cook about 8 minutes or until vegetables are softened and onion is translucent, stirring occasionally.

2. Whisk in flour; cook and stir 1 minute. Whisk in half-and-half; cook about 15 minutes or until thickened, stirring occasionally.

3. Whisk in broth, salt, thyme, parsley flakes and nutmeg; cook 10 minutes or until soup is slightly thickened, stirring occasionally. Add gnocchi, chicken, carrots and spinach; cook about 5 minutes or until gnocchi are heated through.

HOT AND SOUR SOUP

MAKES 4 TO 6 SERVINGS

INSPIRED BY PEI WEI®

- 1 package (1 ounce) dried shiitake mushrooms
- 4 ounces firm tofu, drained
- 4 cups chicken broth
- 3 tablespoons white vinegar
- 2 tablespoons soy sauce
- ½ to 1 teaspoon hot chili oil
- 1 teaspoon white pepper, divided
- 1 cup shredded cooked chicken
- ½ cup drained canned bamboo shoots, cut into thin strips
- 3 tablespoons water
- 2 tablespoons cornstarch
- 1 egg white, lightly beaten
- 2 tablespoons balsamic vinegar
- 1 teaspoon dark sesame oil
- ¼ cup thinly sliced green onions (optional)

1. Place mushrooms in small bowl; cover with warm water and let stand 20 minutes to soften. Drain mushrooms; squeeze out excess water. Discard stems; slice caps. Press tofu lightly between paper towels; cut into ½-inch cubes.

2. Combine broth, white vinegar, soy sauce, chili oil and ½ teaspoon white pepper in large saucepan; bring to a boil over high heat. Reduce heat to medium-low; cook 2 minutes. Add mushrooms, tofu, chicken and bamboo shoots; cook and stir 5 minutes or until heated through.

3. Stir 3 tablespoons water into cornstarch in small bowl until smooth. Stir into soup; cook 4 minutes or until soup boils and thickens, stirring frequently.

4. Remove from heat. Stirring constantly in one direction, slowly pour egg white in thin stream into soup. Stir in balsamic vinegar, sesame oil and remaining ½ teaspoon white pepper. Garnish with green onions.

SAUSAGE RICE SOUP

MAKES 4 TO 6 SERVINGS

- 2 teaspoons olive oil
- 8 ounces Italian sausage, casings removed
- 1 small onion, chopped
- ½ teaspoon fennel seeds
- 1 tablespoon tomato paste
- 4 cups chicken broth
- 1 can (about 14 ounces) whole tomatoes, undrained, crushed with hands or coarsely chopped
- 1½ cups water
- ½ cup uncooked rice
- ¼ teaspoon salt
- ⅛ teaspoon black pepper
- 2 to 3 ounces baby spinach
- ⅓ cup shredded mozzarella cheese (optional)

1. Heat oil in large saucepan or Dutch oven over medium-high heat. Add sausage; cook 8 minutes or until browned, stirring to break up meat. Add onion; cook and stir 5 minutes or until softened. Add fennel seeds; cook and stir 30 seconds. Add tomato paste; cook and stir 1 minute.

2. Stir in broth, tomatoes with juice, water, rice, ¼ teaspoon salt and ⅛ teaspoon pepper; bring to a boil. Reduce heat to medium-low; cook 18 minutes or until rice is tender.

3. Stir in spinach; cook 3 minutes or until wilted. Season with additional salt and pepper.

4. Sprinkle with cheese, if desired, just before serving.

WEDGE SALAD

MAKES 4 SERVINGS

INSPIRED BY
LONE STAR
STEAKHOUSE

DRESSING

- ¾ cup mayonnaise
- ½ cup buttermilk
- 1 cup crumbled blue cheese, divided
- 1 clove garlic, minced
- ½ teaspoon sugar
- ⅛ teaspoon onion powder
- ⅛ teaspoon salt
- ⅛ teaspoon black pepper

SALAD

- 1 head iceberg lettuce
- 1 large tomato, diced (about 1 cup)
- ½ small red onion, cut into thin rings
- ½ cup crumbled crisp-cooked bacon (6 to 8 slices)

1. For dressing, combine mayonnaise, buttermilk, ½ cup cheese, garlic, sugar, onion powder, salt and pepper in food processor or blender; process until smooth.

2. For salad, cut lettuce into quarters through stem end; remove stem from each wedge.

3. Place wedges on individual serving plates; top with dressing. Sprinkle with tomato, onion, remaining ½ cup cheese and bacon.

CHICKEN WALDORF SALAD

MAKES 4 SERVINGS

DRESSING

- ⅓ cup balsamic vinegar
- 2 tablespoons Dijon mustard
- 2 teaspoons minced garlic
- ½ teaspoon salt
- ¼ teaspoon black pepper
- ⅔ cup extra virgin olive oil

SALAD

- 8 cups mixed greens
- 1 large Granny Smith apple, cut into ½-inch pieces
- ⅔ cup diced celery
- ⅔ cup halved red seedless grapes
- 12 to 16 ounces grilled chicken breast strips
- ½ cup candied walnuts*
- ½ cup crumbled blue cheese

Glazed or candied walnuts may be found in the produce section of the supermarket with other salad toppings, or they may be found in the snack aisle.

1. For dressing, combine vinegar, mustard, garlic, salt and pepper in medium bowl; mix well. Slowly add oil, whisking until well blended.

2. For salad, combine mixed greens, apple, celery and grapes in large bowl. Add half of dressing; toss to coat. Top with chicken, walnuts and cheese; drizzle with additional dressing.

GREEN GODDESS COBB SALAD

MAKES 4 SERVINGS

PICKLED ONIONS

- 1 cup thinly sliced red onion
- ½ cup white wine vinegar
- ¼ cup water
- 2 teaspoons sugar
- 1 teaspoon salt

DRESSING

- 1 cup mayonnaise
- 1 cup fresh Italian parsley leaves
- 1 cup baby arugula
- ¼ cup extra virgin olive oil
- 3 tablespoons lemon juice
- 3 tablespoons minced fresh chives
- 2 tablespoons fresh tarragon leaves
- 1 clove garlic, minced
- 1 teaspoon Dijon mustard
- ½ teaspoon salt
- ⅛ teaspoon black pepper

SALAD

- 4 eggs
- 4 cups Italian salad blend (romaine and radicchio)
- 2 cups chopped stemmed kale
- 2 cups baby arugula
- 2 avocados, halved and sliced
- 2 tomatoes, cut into wedges
- 2 cups grilled or roasted chicken breast strips
- 1 cup chopped crisp-cooked bacon

1. For pickled onions, combine onion, vinegar, ¼ cup water, sugar and 1 teaspoon salt in large glass jar. Seal jar; shake well. Refrigerate at least 1 hour or up to 1 week.

2. For dressing, combine mayonnaise, parsley, 1 cup arugula, oil, lemon juice, chives, tarragon, garlic, mustard, ½ teaspoon salt and pepper in blender or food processor; blend until smooth, stopping to scrape down side once or twice. Transfer to jar; refrigerate until ready to use. Just before serving, thin dressing with 1 to 2 tablespoons water, if necessary, to reach desired consistency.

3. Fill medium saucepan with water; bring to a boil over high heat. Carefully lower eggs into water. Reduce heat to medium; boil gently 12 minutes. Drain eggs; add cold water and ice cubes to saucepan to cool eggs. When eggs are cool enough to handle, peel and cut in half lengthwise.

4. Combine salad blend, kale, 2 cups arugula and pickled onions in large bowl; divide among four individual serving bowls. Top each salad with avocados, tomatoes, chicken, bacon and two egg halves. Top with ¼ cup dressing; toss to coat.

SHRIMP AND SPINACH SALAD

MAKES 4 SERVINGS

DRESSING

- 3 to 4 slices bacon
- ¼ cup red wine vinegar
- ½ teaspoon cornstarch
- ¼ cup olive oil
- ¼ cup sugar
- ¼ teaspoon salt
- ¼ teaspoon black pepper
- ¼ teaspoon liquid smoke

SHRIMP

- 2 teaspoons black pepper
- 1 teaspoon salt
- 1 teaspoon garlic powder
- ½ teaspoon sugar
- ½ teaspoon onion powder
- ½ teaspoon ground sage
- ½ teaspoon paprika
- 20 to 24 large raw shrimp, peeled and deveined
- 2 tablespoons olive oil

SALAD

- 8 cups packed torn stemmed spinach
- 1 tomato, diced
- ½ red onion, thinly sliced
- ½ cup sliced roasted red peppers

1. For dressing, cook bacon in large skillet over medium heat until crisp. Drain on paper towel-lined plate. Crumble bacon; set aside.

2. Heat skillet with drippings over medium heat. Stir vinegar into cornstarch in small bowl until smooth. Whisk cornstarch mixture into drippings in skillet; cook 1 to 2 minutes or until slightly thickened, whisking constantly. Remove from heat; pour into small bowl or glass measuring cup. Whisk in ¼ cup oil, ¼ cup sugar, ¼ teaspoon salt, ¼ teaspoon black pepper and liquid smoke until well blended. Wipe out skillet with paper towel.

3. For shrimp, combine 2 teaspoons black pepper, 1 teaspoon salt, garlic powder, ½ teaspoon sugar, onion powder, sage and paprika in medium bowl; mix well. Add shrimp; toss to coat.

4. Heat 2 tablespoons oil in same skillet over medium-high heat. Add shrimp; cook 2 to 3 minutes per side or until shrimp are pink and opaque.

5. For salad, combine spinach, tomato, onion and roasted peppers in large bowl. Add two thirds of dressing; toss to coat. Top with shrimp and crumbled bacon; serve with remaining dressing.

PECAN-CRUSTED CHICKEN SALAD

INSPIRED BY TGI FRIDAYS℠

MAKES 4 SERVINGS

114

salads

CHICKEN

- ½ cup all-purpose flour
- ½ cup milk
- 1 egg
- ⅔ cup corn flake crumbs
- ⅔ cup finely chopped pecans
- ¾ teaspoon salt
- 4 boneless skinless chicken breasts (1¼ to 1½ pounds total)

DRESSING

- ⅓ cup balsamic vinegar
- 1 tablespoon Dijon mustard
- 1 tablespoon sugar
- 1 teaspoon minced garlic
- ½ teaspoon salt
- ⅔ cup canola oil

SALAD

- 10 cups mixed greens (1-pound package)
- 2 cans (11 ounces each) mandarin oranges, drained
- 1 cup sliced celery
- ¾ cup dried cranberries
- ½ cup glazed pecans*
- ½ cup crumbled blue cheese

Glazed or candied pecans may be found in the produce section of the supermarket with other salad toppings, or they may be found in the snack aisle.

1. Preheat oven to 400°F. Line baking sheet with foil; spray with nonstick cooking spray.

2. Place flour in shallow dish. Beat milk and egg in another shallow dish. Combine corn flake crumbs, chopped pecans and ¾ teaspoon salt in third shallow dish. Dip both sides of chicken in flour, then in egg mixture, letting excess drip back into dish. Roll in crumb mixture to coat completely, pressing crumbs into chicken to adhere. Place on prepared baking sheet.

3. Bake 20 minutes or until chicken is cooked through (165°F). Cool completely before slicing. (Chicken can be prepared several hours in advance and refrigerated.)

4. Meanwhile, prepare dressing. Combine vinegar, mustard, sugar, garlic and ½ teaspoon salt in medium bowl; mix well. Slowly add oil, whisking until well blended.

5. For salad, combine mixed greens, mandarin oranges, celery, cranberries, glazed pecans and cheese in large bowl. Add two thirds of dressing; toss gently to coat. Divide salad among four plates. Cut chicken breasts diagonally into ½-inch slices; arrange over salads. Serve with remaining dressing.

STEAKHOUSE CHOPPED SALAD

MAKES 8 TO 10 SERVINGS

DRESSING

Italian Seasoning Mix
(recipe follows)
or 1 package (about
2 tablespoons) Italian
salad dressing mix

⅓ cup white balsamic
vinegar

¼ cup Dijon mustard

⅔ cup extra virgin olive oil

SALAD

1 medium head iceberg
lettuce, chopped

1 medium head romaine
lettuce, chopped

1 can (about 14 ounces)
hearts of palm *or*
artichoke hearts,
quartered lengthwise
then sliced crosswise

1 large avocado, diced

1½ cups crumbled
blue cheese

2 hard-cooked eggs,
chopped

1 ripe tomato, chopped

½ small red onion,
finely chopped

12 slices bacon, crisp-cooked
and crumbled

1. For dressing, prepare Italian Seasoning mix. Whisk vinegar, mustard and dressing mix in small bowl. Slowly add oil, whisking until well blended. Set aside until ready to use. (Dressing can be made up to 1 week in advance; refrigerate in jar with tight-fitting lid.)

2. For salad, combine lettuce, hearts of palm, avocado, cheese, eggs, tomato, onion and bacon in large bowl. Add dressing; toss to coat.

ITALIAN SEASONING MIX

MAKES ABOUT 2½ TABLESPOONS

1½ teaspoons salt

1½ teaspoons dried oregano

¾ teaspoon sugar

¾ teaspoon onion powder

¾ teaspoon dried parsley
flakes

½ teaspoon garlic powder

¼ teaspoon dried basil

¼ teaspoon black pepper

⅛ teaspoon dried thyme

⅛ teaspoon celery salt

Combine all ingredients in small bowl; mix well.

116

salads

BBQ CHICKEN SALAD

MAKES 4 SERVINGS

DRESSING

- ¾ cup light or regular mayonnaise
- ⅓ cup buttermilk
- ¼ cup sour cream
- 1 tablespoon white wine vinegar
- 1 teaspoon sugar
- ¼ teaspoon salt
- ¼ teaspoon garlic powder
- ¼ teaspoon onion powder
- ¼ teaspoon dried parsley flakes
- ¼ teaspoon dried dill weed
- ¼ teaspoon black pepper

SALAD

- 12 to 16 ounces grilled chicken breast strips
- ½ cup barbecue sauce
- 4 cups chopped romaine lettuce
- 4 cups chopped iceberg lettuce
- 2 medium tomatoes, seeded and chopped
- ¾ cup canned or thawed frozen corn, drained
- ¾ cup diced jicama
- ¾ cup (3 ounces) shredded Monterey Jack cheese
- ¼ cup chopped fresh cilantro
- 2 green onions, sliced
- 1 cup crispy tortilla strips*

  *If tortilla strips are unavailable, crumble tortilla chips into bite-size pieces.

1. For dressing, whisk mayonnaise, buttermilk, sour cream, vinegar, sugar, salt, garlic powder, onion powder, parsley flakes, dill weed and pepper in medium bowl until well blended. Cover and refrigerate until ready to serve.

2. For salad, cut chicken strips into ½-inch pieces. Combine chicken and barbecue sauce in medium bowl; toss to coat.

3. Combine lettuce, tomatoes, corn, jicama, cheese and cilantro in large bowl. Add two thirds of dressing; toss to coat. Add remaining dressing, if necessary. Divide salad among four plates; top with chicken, green onions and tortilla strips.

HOUSE SALAD

MAKES 4 SERVINGS

DRESSING

- ½ cup mayonnaise
- ½ cup white wine vinegar
- ¼ cup grated Parmesan cheese
- 1 tablespoon olive oil
- 1 tablespoon lemon juice
- 1 tablespoon corn syrup
- 1 clove garlic, minced
- ¾ teaspoon Italian seasoning
- ½ teaspoon salt
- ½ teaspoon black pepper

SALAD

- 1 package (10 ounces) Italian salad blend
- 2 plum tomatoes, thinly sliced
- 1 cup croutons
- ½ cup thinly sliced red or green bell pepper
- ½ cup thinly sliced red onion
- ¼ cup sliced black olives
  Pepperoncini (optional)

1. For dressing, whisk mayonnaise, vinegar, cheese, oil, lemon juice, corn syrup, garlic, Italian seasoning, salt and black pepper in medium bowl until well blended.

2. For salad, place salad blend in large bowl; top with tomatoes, croutons, bell pepper, onion, olives and pepperoncini, if desired. Add dressing; toss to coat.

AUTUMN HARVEST SALAD

MAKES 6 SERVINGS

DRESSING

- ½ cup extra virgin olive oil
- 3 tablespoons balsamic vinegar
- 1 clove garlic, minced
- 1 teaspoon honey
- 1 teaspoon Dijon mustard
- ½ teaspoon dried oregano
- ½ teaspoon salt
- ⅛ teaspoon black pepper

SALAD

- 1 loaf (12 to 16 ounces) artisan pecan raisin bread
- 4 tablespoons (½ stick) butter, melted
- 6 tablespoons coarse sugar (such as demerara, turbinado or organic cane sugar)
- 6 cups packed spring greens
- 2 Granny Smith apples, thinly sliced
- 18 to 24 ounces grilled chicken breast strips
- ¾ cup crumbled blue cheese
- ¾ cup dried cranberries
- ¾ cup toasted walnuts*

  To toast walnuts, spread on ungreased baking sheet. Bake in preheated 350°F oven 6 to 8 minutes or until lightly browned, stirring frequently.

1. For dressing, whisk oil, vinegar, garlic, honey, mustard, oregano, salt and pepper in medium bowl until well blended. Refrigerate until ready to use.

2. Preheat oven to 350°F. Line baking sheet with parchment paper. Cut bread into thin (¼-inch) slices; place in single layer on prepared baking sheet. Brush one side of each slice with melted butter; sprinkle each slice with ½ teaspoon sugar. Bake 10 minutes. Turn slices; brush with butter and sprinkle with ½ teaspoon sugar. Bake 10 minutes. Cool completely on baking sheet.

3. For each salad, place 1 cup greens on serving plate. Top with ½ cup apple slices, ¼ cup chicken strips and 2 tablespoons each cheese, cranberries and walnuts. Break 2 toast slices into pieces and sprinkle over salad. Drizzle with 2 tablespoons dressing.

MEDITERRANEAN SALAD

MAKES 4 SERVINGS

- 2 cups chopped iceberg lettuce
- 2 cups baby spinach
- 2 cups diced cucumbers
- 1 cup diced cooked chicken
- 1 cup chopped roasted red peppers
- 1 cup grape tomatoes, halved
- 1 cup quartered artichoke hearts
- ¾ cup crumbled feta cheese
- ½ cup chopped red onion
- 1 cup hummus
- ½ teaspoon Italian seasoning

1. Divide lettuce and spinach among four salad bowls or plates; top with cucumbers, chicken, roasted peppers, tomatoes, artichokes, cheese and onion.

2. Top salad with hummus; sprinkle with Italian seasoning.

STRAWBERRY POPPY SEED CHICKEN SALAD

INSPIRED BY PANERA BREAD®

MAKES 4 SERVINGS

DRESSING

- ¼ cup white wine vinegar
- 2 tablespoons orange juice
- 1 tablespoon sugar
- 2 teaspoons poppy seeds
- 1½ teaspoons Dijon mustard
- ½ teaspoon salt
- ½ teaspoon minced dried onion
- ½ cup vegetable oil

SALAD

- 8 cups romaine lettuce
- 12 to 16 ounces grilled chicken breast strips
- ¾ cup fresh pineapple chunks
- ¾ cup sliced fresh strawberries
- ¾ cup fresh blueberries
- 1 navel orange, peeled and sectioned *or* 1 can (11 ounces) mandarin oranges, drained
- ¼ cup chopped toasted pecans

1. For dressing, combine vinegar, orange juice, sugar, poppy seeds, mustard, salt and dried onion in small bowl; mix well. Slowly whisk in oil in thin, steady stream until well blended.

2. For salad, combine romaine and two thirds of dressing in large bowl; toss gently to coat. Divide salad among four plates, top with chicken, pineapple, strawberries, blueberries, oranges and pecans. Serve with remaining dressing.

TACO SALAD SUPREME

MAKES 4 SERVINGS

INSPIRED BY WENDY'S®

salads

CHILI

- 1 pound ground beef
- 1 medium onion, chopped
- 1 stalk celery, chopped
- 2 medium fresh tomatoes, chopped
- 1 jalapeño pepper,* finely chopped
- 1½ teaspoons chili powder
- 1 teaspoon salt
- 1 teaspoon ground cumin
- ½ teaspoon black pepper
- 1 can (15 ounces) tomato sauce
- 1 can (about 15 ounces) kidney beans, rinsed and drained
- 1 can (about 15 ounces) pinto beans, rinsed and drained
- 1 cup water

SALAD

- 8 cups chopped romaine lettuce (large pieces)
- 2 cups diced fresh tomatoes
- 48 small round tortilla chips
- 1 cup salsa
- ½ cup sour cream
- ½ cup (2 ounces) shredded Cheddar cheese

Jalapeño peppers can sting and irritate the skin, so wear rubber gloves when handling peppers and do not touch your eyes.

1. For chili, combine beef, onion and celery in large saucepan; cook over medium-high heat 6 to 8 minutes or until beef is no longer pink, stirring to break up meat. Drain fat.

2. Add chopped tomatoes, jalapeño, chili powder, salt, cumin and black pepper; cook and stir 1 minute. Stir in tomato sauce, beans and water; bring to a boil. Reduce heat to medium-low; cook about 1 hour or until most of liquid is absorbed.

3. For each salad, combine 2 cups lettuce and ½ cup diced tomatoes in individual bowl. Top with 12 tortilla chips, ¾ cup chili, ¼ cup salsa and 2 tablespoons sour cream. Sprinkle with 2 tablespoons cheese. (Reserve remaining chili for another use.)

SUPERFOOD KALE SALAD

MAKES 4 SERVINGS

INSPIRED BY FIRST WATCH®, THE DAYTIME CAFE

MAPLE-ROASTED CARROTS

- 8 carrots, trimmed
- 2 tablespoons olive oil
- 2 tablespoons maple syrup
- ½ teaspoon salt
- ⅛ teaspoon black pepper
  Dash ground red pepper

MAPLE-LEMON VINAIGRETTE

- ¼ cup extra virgin olive oil
- 3 tablespoons lemon juice
- 2 tablespoons maple syrup
- ¾ teaspoon grated lemon peel
- ½ teaspoon salt
- ⅛ teaspoon black pepper

SALAD

- 4 cups chopped kale
- 2 cups chopped mixed greens
- 1 cup dried cranberries
- 1 cup slivered almonds, toasted*
- 1 cup shredded Parmesan cheese
- 12 to 16 ounces grilled chicken breast strips

To toast almonds, spread on ungreased baking sheet. Bake in preheated 350°F oven 6 to 8 minutes or until lightly browned, stirring occasionally.

1. Preheat oven to 400°F. Line baking sheet with parchment paper.

2. Place carrots on prepared baking sheet. Whisk 2 tablespoons oil, 2 tablespoons maple syrup, ½ teaspoon salt, ⅛ teaspoon black pepper and red pepper in small bowl until well blended. Brush some of oil mixture over carrots. Roast 30 minutes or until carrots are tender, brushing with oil mixture and shaking baking sheet every 10 minutes. Cut carrots crosswise into ¼-inch slices when cool enough to handle.

3. While carrots are roasting, prepare vinaigrette. Whisk ¼ cup oil, lemon juice, 2 tablespoons maple syrup, lemon peel, ½ teaspoon salt and ⅛ teaspoon black pepper in small bowl until well blended.

4. Combine kale, greens, cranberries, almonds and cheese in large bowl. Add carrots. Pour vinaigrette over salad; toss to coat. Top with chicken.

GARBAGE SALAD

MAKES 4 TO 6 SERVINGS

DRESSING

- ⅓ cup red wine vinegar
- 2 cloves garlic, minced
- 2 teaspoons sugar
- 1 teaspoon Italian seasoning
- ¼ teaspoon salt
- ¼ teaspoon black pepper
- ⅓ cup vegetable or canola oil

SALAD

- 1 package (5 ounces) spring mix
- 5 romaine lettuce leaves, chopped
- 1 small cucumber, diced
- 2 small plum tomatoes, diced
- ½ red onion, thinly sliced
- ¼ cup pitted kalamata olives
- 4 radishes, thinly sliced
- 4 ounces thinly sliced Genoa salami, cut into ¼-inch strips
- 4 ounces provolone cheese, cut into ¼-inch strips
- ¼ cup grated Parmesan cheese

1. For dressing, whisk vinegar, garlic, sugar, Italian seasoning, salt and pepper in small bowl until blended. Slowly whisk in oil in thin, steady stream until well blended.

2. For salad, combine spring mix, romaine, cucumber, tomatoes, onion, olives and radishes in large bowl. Add half of dressing; toss gently to coat. Top with salami and provolone; sprinkle with Parmesan. Serve with remaining dressing.

salads

SPINACH SALAD

MAKES 4 SERVINGS

salads

DRESSING

- ¼ cup balsamic vinegar
- 1 clove garlic, minced
- ½ teaspoon sugar
- ¼ teaspoon salt
- ⅛ teaspoon black pepper
- ¼ cup olive oil
- ¼ cup vegetable oil

SALAD

- 8 cups packed baby spinach
- 1 cup diced tomatoes (about 2 medium)
- 1 cup drained mandarin oranges
- 1 cup glazed pecans*
- ½ cup crumbled feta cheese
- ½ cup diced red onion
- ½ cup dried cranberries
- 1 can (3 ounces) crispy rice noodles**
- 4 teaspoons toasted sesame seeds

*Glazed or candied pecans can be found in the produce section of the supermarket along with other salad toppings, or they may be found in the snack aisle. If unavailable, they can be prepared easily at home. (See Tip.)

**Crispy rice noodles can be found with canned chow mein noodles in the Asian section of the supermarket.

1. For dressing, whisk vinegar, garlic, sugar, salt and pepper in medium bowl until blended. Slowly whisk in olive oil and vegetable oil in thin, steady stream until well blended.

2. For salad, divide spinach among four serving bowls. Top with tomatoes, mandarin oranges, pecans, cheese, onion and cranberries. Sprinkle with rice noodles and sesame seeds. Drizzle each salad with 3 tablespoons dressing.

tip

To make glazed pecans, combine 1 cup pecan halves, ¼ cup sugar, 1 tablespoon butter and ½ teaspoon salt in medium skillet; cook and stir over medium heat 5 minutes or until sugar mixture is dark brown and nuts are well coated. Spread on large plate; cool completely. Break into pieces or coarsely chop.

AMAZING APPLE SALAD

MAKES 4 SERVINGS (1 CUP DRESSING)

DRESSING

- 5 tablespoons apple juice concentrate
- ¼ cup white balsamic vinegar
- 1 tablespoon lemon juice
- 1 tablespoon sugar
- 1 clove garlic, minced
- ½ teaspoon salt
- ½ teaspoon onion powder
- ¼ teaspoon ground ginger
- ¼ cup extra virgin olive oil

SALAD

- 12 cups mixed greens such as chopped romaine lettuce and spring greens
- 12 ounces thinly sliced cooked chicken
- 2 tomatoes, cut into wedges
- 1 package (about 3 ounces) dried apple chips
- ½ red onion, thinly sliced
- ½ cup crumbled gorgonzola or blue cheese
- ½ cup pecans, toasted*

To toast pecans, cook in small skillet over medium heat 1 to 2 minutes or until lightly browned, stirring frequently.

1. For dressing, whisk apple juice concentrate, vinegar, lemon juice, sugar, garlic, salt, onion powder and ginger in small bowl until blended. Slowly whisk in oil in thin, steady stream until well blended.

2. For salad, divide greens among four serving bowls. Top with chicken, tomatoes, apple chips, onion, cheese and pecans.

3. Drizzle about 2 tablespoons dressing over each salad.

ROASTED BRUSSELS SPROUTS SALAD

MAKES 6 SERVINGS

BRUSSELS SPROUTS

1 pound brussels sprouts, trimmed and halved

2 tablespoons olive oil

½ teaspoon salt

SALAD

2 cups coarsely chopped baby kale

2 cups coarsely chopped romaine lettuce

1½ cups candied pecans*

1 cup halved red grapes

1 cup diced cucumbers

½ cup dried cranberries

½ cup fresh blueberries

½ cup chopped red onion

¼ cup toasted pumpkin seeds (pepitas)

1 container (4 ounces) crumbled goat cheese

DRESSING

½ cup olive oil

6 tablespoons balsamic vinegar

6 tablespoons strawberry jam

2 teaspoons Dijon mustard

1 teaspoon salt

*Glazed or candied pecans may be found in the produce section of the supermarket with other salad toppings, or they may be found in the snack aisle.

1. For brussels sprouts, preheat oven to 400°F. Spray large baking sheet with nonstick cooking spray.

2. Combine brussels sprouts, 2 tablespoons oil and ½ teaspoon salt in medium bowl; toss to coat. Arrange brussels sprouts in single layer, cut sides down, on prepared baking sheet. Roast 20 minutes or until tender and browned, stirring once halfway through roasting. Cool completely on baking sheet.

3. For salad, combine kale, lettuce, pecans, grapes, cucumbers, cranberries, blueberries, onion and pumpkin seeds in large bowl. Top with brussels sprouts and cheese.

4. For dressing, whisk ½ cup oil, vinegar, jam, mustard and 1 teaspoon salt in small bowl until well blended. Pour dressing over salad; toss gently to coat.

sandwiches

INSPIRED BY TGI FRIDAYS℠

TUSCAN PORTOBELLO MELT

MAKES 2 SERVINGS

- 1 portobello mushroom cap, thinly sliced
- ½ small red onion, thinly sliced
- ½ cup grape tomatoes
- 1 tablespoon olive oil
- 1 teaspoon balsamic vinegar
- ⅛ teaspoon salt
- ⅛ teaspoon dried thyme
- ⅛ teaspoon black pepper
- 2 tablespoons butter, softened and divided
- 4 slices sourdough bread
- 2 slices provolone cheese
- 2 teaspoons Dijon mustard
- 2 slices Monterey Jack cheese

1. Preheat broiler. Combine mushroom, onion and tomatoes in small baking pan. Drizzle with oil and vinegar; sprinkle with salt, thyme and pepper. Toss to coat. Spread vegetables in single layer in pan.

2. Broil 6 minutes or until vegetables are softened and browned, stirring once.

3. Heat medium skillet over medium heat. Spread 1 tablespoon butter over one side of each bread slice. Place buttered side down in skillet; cook 2 minutes or until bread is toasted. Transfer bread to cutting board, toasted sides up.

4. Place provolone cheese on 2 bread slices; spread mustard over cheese. Top with vegetables, Monterey Jack cheese and remaining bread slices, toasted sides down. Spread remaining 1 tablespoon butter on outside of sandwiches. Cook in same skillet over medium heat 5 minutes or until bread is toasted and cheese is melted, turning once.

CUBAN PORK SANDWICH

MAKES 4 SERVINGS

- ⅓ cup orange juice
- 3 tablespoons lime juice
- 1 small onion, finely chopped (½ cup)
- 3 tablespoons olive oil
- 6 cloves garlic, minced
- 2 teaspoons ground cumin
- 2 teaspoons dried oregano
- 1 teaspoon salt
- 1 teaspoon black pepper
- 2 pounds boneless pork shoulder
- 4 Cuban sandwich rolls, split*
- ⅓ cup mayonnaise
- ⅓ cup yellow mustard
- 8 ounces sliced Swiss cheese
- 8 ounces sliced honey ham
- 8 long thin dill pickle slices

If Cuban rolls are unavailable, substitute a long French or Italian loaf, split in half horizontally and cut into 4 pieces.

1. Combine orange juice, lime juice, onion, oil, garlic, cumin, oregano, salt and pepper in medium bowl; mix well. Place pork in large resealable food storage bag. Pour marinade over pork; seal bag and turn to coat. Marinate in refrigerator at least 2 hours or overnight.

2. Preheat oven to 325°F. Line shallow roasting pan or baking dish with heavy-duty foil. Place pork in prepared pan with half of marinade; discard remaining marinade. Roast about 3 hours or until pork is tender and temperature reaches 160°F. Let stand at least 15 minutes before slicing. (Pork can be prepared in advance and refrigerated.)

3. Slice pork. (About half of pork is needed for sandwiches; reserve remaining pork for another use.) Spread both cut sides of rolls with mayonnaise, then mustard. Top bottom halves of rolls with half of cheese, ham, pickles, pork, remaining cheese and top halves of rolls.

4. Cook sandwiches in sandwich press, grill pan or hot skillet over medium heat until bread is browned and crisp. (If using grill pan or skillet, use second skillet to press down and compress sandwiches; cook about 5 minutes per side until bread is crisp.)

TOMATO MOZZARELLA SANDWICH

MAKES 4 SERVINGS

BALSAMIC VINAIGRETTE

- 6 tablespoons extra virgin olive oil
- 3 tablespoons balsamic vinegar
- 1 clove garlic, minced
- 1 teaspoon honey
- 1 teaspoon Dijon mustard
- ½ teaspoon dried oregano
- ½ teaspoon salt
- ⅛ teaspoon black pepper

SANDWICHES

- 1 baguette, ends trimmed, cut into 4 equal pieces (4 ounces each) and split
- 1 cup loosely packed baby arugula
- 3 medium tomatoes, sliced ¼ inch thick
- 1 cup roasted red peppers, patted dry and thinly sliced
- 12 slices fresh mozzarella (one 8-ounce package)
- 12 fresh basil leaves

1. For vinaigrette, whisk oil, vinegar, garlic, honey, mustard, oregano, salt and pepper in small bowl until well blended.

2. For each sandwich, drizzle 1 tablespoon vinaigrette over bottom half of bread. Layer with arugula, tomatoes, roasted peppers, cheese slices, additional arugula and basil. Drizzle with 1 tablespoon dressing; replace top half of bread.

GUACAMOLE BURGERS

MAKES 4 SERVINGS

- 1 small avocado
- 2 tablespoons finely chopped tomato
- 1 tablespoon chopped fresh cilantro
- 2 teaspoons lime juice, divided
- 1 teaspoon minced jalapeño pepper*
- ¼ teaspoon salt, divided
- 2 tablespoons sour cream
- 2 tablespoons mayonnaise
- ½ teaspoon ground cumin
- 4 teaspoons vegetable oil, divided
- 1 medium onion, cut into thin slices
- 1 small green bell pepper, cut into thin slices
- 1 small red bell pepper, cut into thin slices
- 1¼ pounds ground beef
- Salt and black pepper
- 4 slices Monterey Jack cheese
- 4 hamburger buns, split and toasted
- 1 can (4 ounces) diced fire-roasted jalapeño peppers, drained

Jalapeño peppers can sting and irritate the skin, so wear rubber gloves when handling peppers and do not touch your eyes.

1. Mash avocado in medium bowl. Stir in tomato, cilantro, 1 teaspoon lime juice, minced jalapeño and ⅛ teaspoon salt; mix well. Cover and refrigerate until ready to use. Combine sour cream, mayonnaise, remaining 1 teaspoon lime juice and cumin in small bowl; mix well. Cover and refrigerate until ready to use.

2. Heat 2 teaspoons oil in large skillet over medium-high heat. Add onion; cook about 8 minutes or until onion is very tender and begins to turn golden, stirring occasionally. (Add a few teaspoons water to skillet if onion begins to burn.) Remove to bowl. Add remaining 2 teaspoons oil to skillet. Add bell peppers; cook and stir 5 minutes or until tender. Remove to bowl with onion; season vegetables with remaining ⅛ teaspoon salt.

3. Preheat grill or broiler. Shape beef into four 5-inch patties; sprinkle both sides generously with salt and black pepper. Grill or broil patties about 5 minutes per side or until cooked through (160°F). Top each burger with cheese slice during last minute of cooking.

4. Spread sour cream mixture over bottom halves of buns. Top with vegetables, burgers, guacamole, fire-roasted jalapeños and top halves of buns.

INSPIRED BY PANERA BREAD®

SOUTHWEST TURKEY SANDWICH

MAKES 4 SERVINGS

- ½ cup mayonnaise
- 1 tablespoon minced chipotle pepper in adobo sauce
- 1½ teaspoons lime juice
- 1 round loaf (16 ounces) cheese focaccia or cheese bread (preferably Asiago cheese)
- 1½ cups mixed greens
- 12 ounces sliced smoked turkey
- ½ red onion, thinly sliced

1. Combine mayonnaise, chipotle pepper and lime juice in small bowl; mix well.

2. Cut loaf in half horizontally; spread cut sides of bread with mayonnaise mixture. Top bottom half of loaf with mixed greens, turkey, onion and top half of bread. Cut into wedges.

BLT SUPREME

MAKES 2 SERVINGS

12 to 16 slices thick-cut bacon

⅓ cup mayonnaise

1½ teaspoons minced chipotle pepper in adobo sauce

1 teaspoon lime juice

1 ripe avocado

⅛ teaspoon salt

⅛ teaspoon black pepper

4 leaves romaine lettuce

½ baguette, cut into 2 (8-inch) lengths *or* 2 hoagie rolls, split and toasted

6 to 8 slices tomato

1. Cook bacon in skillet or oven until crisp-chewy. Drain on paper towel-lined plate.

2. Meanwhile, combine mayonnaise, chipotle pepper and lime juice in small bowl; mix well. Coarsely mash avocado in another small bowl; stir in salt and black pepper. Cut romaine leaves crosswise into ¼-inch strips.

3. For each sandwich, spread heaping tablespoon mayonnaise mixture on bottom half of baguette; top with one fourth of lettuce. Arrange 3 to 4 bacon slices over lettuce; spread 2 tablespoons mashed avocado over bacon. Drizzle with heaping tablespoon mayonnaise mixture. Top with 3 to 4 tomato slices, one fourth of lettuce and 3 to 4 bacon slices. Close sandwich with top half of baguette.

ALMOND CHICKEN SALAD SANDWICH

MAKES 4 SERVINGS

¼ cup mayonnaise

¼ cup plain Greek yogurt
   or sour cream

2 tablespoons cider vinegar

1 tablespoon honey

1 teaspoon salt

½ teaspoon black pepper

⅛ teaspoon garlic powder

2 cups chopped cooked
   chicken

¾ cup halved red grapes

1 large stalk celery, chopped

⅓ cup sliced almonds

   Leaf lettuce

1 tomato, thinly sliced

8 slices sesame semolina or
   country Italian bread

1. Whisk mayonnaise, yogurt, vinegar, honey, salt, pepper and garlic powder in small bowl until well blended.

2. Combine chicken, grapes and celery in medium bowl. Add dressing; toss gently to coat. Cover and refrigerate several hours or overnight. Stir in almonds just before making sandwiches.

3. Place lettuce and tomato slices on 4 bread slices; top with chicken salad and remaining bread slices. Serve immediately.

sandwiches

DOUBLE DECKER TACOS

MAKES 8 TACOS

- 2 tablespoons all-purpose flour
- 2 teaspoons chili powder
- 1 teaspoon dried minced onion
- ¾ teaspoon paprika
- ½ teaspoon salt
- ½ teaspoon garlic powder
- ¼ teaspoon sugar
- 1 pound ground beef
- ⅔ cup water
- 8 taco shells
- 8 mini (5-inch) flour tortillas*
- 2 cups refried beans, warmed
- 1 cup shredded romaine lettuce
- 1 cup chopped tomato
- 1 cup (4 ounces) shredded Cheddar cheese

  Sour cream (optional)

  Mini flour tortillas may also be labeled as street tacos.

INSPIRED BY TACO BELL®

1. Preheat oven to 350°F. Combine flour, chili powder, onion, paprika, salt, garlic powder and sugar in small bowl; mix well.

2. Cook beef in large skillet over medium-high heat 6 to 8 minutes or until browned, stirring to break up meat. Drain fat. Add flour mixture; cook and stir 2 minutes. Stir in water; bring to a simmer. Reduce heat to medium; cook about 10 minutes or until most of liquid has evaporated. Meanwhile, heat taco shells in oven about 5 minutes or until warm.

3. Wrap tortillas in damp paper towel; microwave on HIGH 25 to 35 seconds or until warm. Spread each tortilla with ¼ cup refried beans, leaving ¼-inch border around edge. Wrap flour tortillas around outside of taco shells, pressing gently to seal together.

4. Fill taco shells with beef mixture; top with lettuce, tomato and cheese. Drizzle with sour cream, if desired. Serve immediately.

BLACKENED CHICKEN TORTA

MAKES 4 SERVINGS

sandwiches

- 2 tablespoons vegetable oil
- 1½ tablespoons Creole seasoning
- 4 boneless skinless chicken breasts (about 6 ounces each)
- ½ cup sour cream
- 2 teaspoons lime juice, divided
- ½ teaspoon ground cumin
- ¼ teaspoon salt, divided
  Dash black pepper
- ⅓ cup mayonnaise
- ½ teaspoon chipotle chili powder
- 1 ripe avocado
- 4 slices Cheddar cheese (about 1 ounce each)
- 4 slices pepper Jack cheese (about 1 ounce each)
- 4 ciabatta rolls, split
- 1 cup finely shredded green cabbage or coleslaw mix

1. Combine oil and Creole seasoning in shallow dish; mix well. Add chicken; turn to coat completely with spice mixture. Let stand while preparing sauces.

2. Combine sour cream, 1½ teaspoons lime juice, cumin, ⅛ teaspoon salt and dash of pepper in medium bowl; mix well. Combine mayonnaise, remaining ½ teaspoon lime juice, ⅛ teaspoon salt and chipotle chili powder in small bowl; mix well. Mash avocado in another small bowl; season with additional salt and pepper.

3. Heat cast iron skillet over medium-high heat until very hot. Add chicken to hot skillet; cook about 6 minutes per side or until well browned and cooked through (165°F). Remove to plate; top each chicken breast with 1 slice Cheddar and 1 slice pepper Jack cheese. Tent loosely with foil to melt cheese.

4. For each sandwich, spread 2 tablespoons sour cream mixture on bottom half of roll; top with mashed avocado. Layer with ¼ cup cabbage and cheese-topped chicken breast. Spread heaping tablespoon mayonnaise mixture on top half of roll; close sandwich.

CLASSIC PATTY MELTS

MAKES 4 SERVINGS

5 tablespoons butter, divided

2 large yellow onions, thinly sliced

¾ teaspoon plus pinch salt, divided

1 pound ground chuck (80% lean)

½ teaspoon garlic powder

½ teaspoon onion powder

¼ teaspoon black pepper

8 slices marble rye bread

½ cup Thousand Island dressing

8 slices deli American or Swiss cheese

1. Melt 2 tablespoons butter in large skillet over medium heat. Add onions and pinch of salt; cook 20 minutes or until onions are very soft and golden brown, stirring occasionally. Remove to small bowl; wipe out skillet with paper towel.

2. Combine beef, remaining ¾ teaspoon salt, garlic powder, onion powder and pepper in medium bowl; mix gently. Shape into four patties about the size and shape of bread slices and ¼ to ½ inch thick.

3. Melt 1 tablespoon butter in same skillet over medium-high heat. Add patties, two at a time; cook 3 minutes or until bottoms are browned, pressing down gently with spatula to form crust. Turn patties; cook 3 minutes or until browned. Remove patties to plate; wipe out skillet with paper towel.

4. Spread one side of each bread slice with dressing. Top 4 bread slices with cheese slice, patty, caramelized onions, another cheese slice and remaining bread slices.

5. Melt 1 tablespoon butter in same skillet over medium heat. Add two sandwiches to skillet; cook 4 minutes or until golden brown, pressing down with spatula to crisp bread. Turn sandwiches; cook 4 minutes or until golden brown and cheese is melted. Repeat with remaining 1 tablespoon butter and sandwiches.

MEDITERRANEAN VEGETABLE SANDWICH

MAKES 4 SANDWICHES

½ cup plain hummus

½ jalapeño pepper, seeded
    and minced*

¼ cup minced fresh cilantro

8 slices whole wheat bread

4 leaves lettuce (leaf or
    Bibb lettuce)

2 tomatoes, thinly sliced

½ cucumber, thinly sliced

½ red onion, thinly sliced

½ cup thinly sliced
    peppadew peppers or
    sweet Italian peppers

4 tablespoons (1 ounce)
    crumbled feta cheese

*Jalapeño peppers can sting
and irritate the skin, so wear
rubber gloves when handling
peppers and do not touch
your eyes.*

1. Combine hummus, jalapeño and cilantro in small bowl; mix well.

2. Spread about 1 tablespoon hummus mixture on one side of each bread slice. Layer half of bread slices with lettuce, tomatoes, cucumber, onion, peppadew peppers and feta; top with remaining bread slices. Serve immediately.

NEW ORLEANS-STYLE MUFFALETTA

MAKES 4 TO 6 SERVINGS

¾ cup pitted green olives

½ cup pitted kalamata olives

½ cup giardiniera
   (Italian-style pickled
   vegetables), drained

2 tablespoons fresh
   parsley leaves

2 tablespoons capers

1 clove garlic, minced

2 tablespoons olive oil

1 tablespoon red wine
   vinegar

1 (8-inch) round Italian loaf
   (16 to 22 ounces)

8 ounces thinly sliced ham

8 ounces thinly sliced
   Genoa salami

6 ounces thinly sliced
   provolone cheese

1. Combine olives, giardiniera, parsley, capers and garlic in food processor; pulse until coarsely chopped and no large pieces remain. Transfer to small bowl; stir in oil and vinegar until well blended. Cover and refrigerate several hours or overnight to blend flavors.

2. Cut bread in half crosswise. Spread two thirds of olive salad over bottom half of bread; layer with ham, salami and cheese. Spread remaining olive salad over cheese; top with top half of bread, pressing down slightly to compress. Wrap sandwich with plastic wrap; let stand 1 hour to blend flavors.

3. To serve sandwich warm, preheat oven to 350°F. Remove plastic wrap; wrap sandwich loosely in foil. Bake 5 to 10 minutes or just until sandwich is slightly warm and cheese begins to melt. Cut into wedges.

CHICKEN AND ROASTED TOMATO PANINI

MAKES 4 SERVINGS

164

sandwiches

- 12 ounces plum tomatoes (about 2 large), cut into ⅛-inch slices
- ½ teaspoon coarse salt, divided
- ¼ teaspoon black pepper, divided
- 2 tablespoons olive oil, divided
- 4 boneless skinless chicken breasts (about 4 ounces each)
- 3 tablespoons butter, softened
- ¼ teaspoon garlic powder
- ¼ cup mayonnaise
- 2 tablespoons pesto sauce
- 8 slices sourdough or rustic Italian bread
- 8 slices (about 1 ounce each) provolone cheese
- ½ cup baby spinach

1. Preheat oven to 400°F. Line baking sheet with parchment paper. Arrange tomato slices in single layer on prepared baking sheet. Sprinkle with ¼ teaspoon salt and ⅛ teaspoon pepper; drizzle with 1 tablespoon oil. Roast 25 minutes or until tomatoes are softened and begin to caramelize around edges.

2. Meanwhile, prepare chicken. If chicken breasts are thicker than ½ inch, pound to ½-inch thickness. Heat remaining 1 tablespoon oil in large skillet over medium-high heat. Season both sides of chicken with remaining ¼ teaspoon salt and ⅛ teaspoon pepper. Add to skillet; cook about 6 minutes per side or until golden brown and cooked through (165°F). Remove to plate; let stand 10 minutes before slicing. Cut diagonally into ½-inch slices.

3. Combine butter and garlic powder in small bowl; mix well. Combine mayonnaise and pesto in another small bowl; mix well.

4. Spread one side of each bread slice with garlic butter. For each sandwich, place 1 bread slice, buttered side down, on plate. Spread with generous 1 tablespoon pesto mayonnaise. Layer with 1 cheese slice, 4 to 5 roasted tomato slices, 4 to 6 spinach leaves, 1 sliced chicken breast, second cheese slice and 4 to 6 spinach leaves. Top with second bread slice, buttered side up.

5. Preheat panini press, indoor grill or grill pan. Cook sandwiches until bread is golden brown and cheese is melted.

HEARTY VEGGIE SANDWICH

MAKES 4 SERVINGS

166

sandwiches

- 1 pound cremini mushrooms, stemmed and thinly sliced (⅛-inch slices)
- 2 tablespoons olive oil, divided
- ¾ teaspoon salt, divided
- ¼ teaspoon black pepper
- 1 medium zucchini, diced (¼-inch pieces, about 2 cups)
- 3 tablespoons butter, softened
- 8 slices artisan whole grain bread
- ¼ cup pesto sauce
- ¼ cup mayonnaise
- 2 cups packed baby spinach
- 4 slices mozzarella cheese

1. Preheat oven to 350°F. Combine mushrooms, 1 tablespoon oil, ½ teaspoon salt and pepper in medium bowl; toss to coat. Spread in single layer on large rimmed baking sheet. Roast 20 minutes or until mushrooms are dark brown and dry, stirring after 10 minutes. Cool on baking sheet.

2. Meanwhile, heat remaining 1 tablespoon oil in large skillet over medium heat. Add zucchini and remaining ¼ teaspoon salt; cook and stir 5 minutes or until zucchini is tender and lightly browned. Transfer to bowl; wipe out skillet with paper towels.

3. Spread butter on one side of each bread slice. Turn over bread. Spread pesto on 4 bread slices; spread mayonnaise on remaining 4 slices. Top pesto-covered slices evenly with mushrooms; layer with spinach, zucchini and cheese. Top with remaining bread slices, mayonnaise side down.

4. Heat same skillet over medium heat. Add sandwiches; cover and cook 2 minutes per side or until bread is toasted, spinach is slightly wilted and cheese is beginning to melt. Serve immediately.

CHICKEN FAJITA ROLL-UPS

MAKES 4 SERVINGS

- 1 cup ranch dressing
- 1 teaspoon chili powder
- 2 tablespoons vegetable oil, divided
- 2 teaspoons lime juice
- 2 teaspoons fajita seasoning mix
- ½ teaspoon chipotle chili powder
- ¼ teaspoon salt
- 4 boneless skinless chicken breasts (about 6 ounces each)
- 4 fajita-size flour tortillas (8 to 9 inches)
- 1 cup (4 ounces) shredded Cheddar cheese
- 1 cup (4 ounces) shredded Monterey Jack cheese
- 3 cups shredded lettuce
- 1 cup pico de gallo

1. Combine ranch dressing and chili powder in small bowl; mix well. Refrigerate until ready to serve.

2. Combine 1 tablespoon oil, lime juice, fajita seasoning mix, chipotle chili powder and salt in small bowl; mix well. Coat both sides of chicken with spice mixture.

3. Heat remaining 1 tablespoon oil in large nonstick skillet or grill pan over medium-high heat. Add chicken; cook about 6 minutes per side or until cooked through (165°F). Remove to plate; let stand 5 minutes before slicing. Cut chicken breasts in half lengthwise, then cut crosswise into ½-inch strips.

4. Wipe out skillet with paper towel. Place one tortilla in skillet; sprinkle with ¼ cup Cheddar and ¼ cup Monterey Jack. Heat over medium heat until cheeses are melted. Remove tortilla to clean work surface or cutting board.

5. Sprinkle ¾ cup shredded lettuce down center of tortilla; top with ¼ cup pico de gallo and one fourth of chicken. Fold bottom of tortilla up over filling, then fold in sides and roll up. Cut in half diagonally. Repeat with remaining tortillas, cheese and fillings. Serve with ranch dipping sauce.

sandwiches

THE GREAT REUBEN SANDWICH

MAKES 2 SANDWICHES

4   slices rye bread

¼   cup Thousand Island
     dressing (see Tip)

8   ounces thinly sliced
     corned beef or pastrami

4   slices Swiss cheese

½   cup sauerkraut, well
     drained

2   tablespoons butter

1. Spread one side of each bread slice with dressing. Top 2 bread slices with corned beef, cheese, sauerkraut and remaining bread slices.

2. Melt butter in large skillet over medium heat. Add sandwiches; press down with spatula or weigh down with small plate. Cook sandwiches 6 minutes per side or until cheese is melted and bread is lightly browned, pressing down with spatula to crisp bread slightly. Serve immediately.

/////////////////////////////////////

tip

For homemade Thousand Island dressing, combine 2 tablespoons mayonnaise, 2 tablespoons sweet pickle relish and 1 tablespoon cocktail sauce.

TUNA SALAD SANDWICH

MAKES 2 SERVINGS

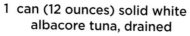

1 can (12 ounces) solid white albacore tuna, drained

1 can (5 ounces) chunk white albacore tuna, drained

¼ cup mayonnaise

1 tablespoon pickle relish

2 teaspoons spicy brown mustard

1 teaspoon lemon juice

½ teaspoon salt

¼ teaspoon black pepper

2 pieces focaccia (about 4×3 inches), split and toasted *or* 4 slices honey wheat bread

Lettuce, tomato and red onion slices

1. Place tuna in medium bowl; flake with fork. Add mayonnaise, pickle relish, mustard, lemon juice, salt and pepper; mix well.

2. Serve tuna salad on focaccia with lettuce, tomato and onion.

172

sandwiches

TURKEY MOZZARELLA PANINI

MAKES 2 TO 4 SERVINGS

BACON JAM

- 1 pound thick-cut bacon, chopped
- 2 large onions, chopped (about 1 pound)
- ⅓ cup packed brown sugar
- ⅛ teaspoon red pepper flakes
- ⅔ cup water
- ¼ cup coffee
- 1½ tablespoons balsamic vinegar

GARLIC AIOLI

- ¼ cup mayonnaise
- 1 clove garlic, minced
- 1 teaspoon lemon juice
- ⅛ teaspoon salt

PANINI

- 2 (6- to 7-inch) round focaccia breads, split
- 2 plum tomatoes, cut into ¼-inch slices
- 6 ounces sliced fresh mozzarella (¼-inch-thick slices)
- 6 ounces thickly sliced turkey breast (about ¼-inch-thick slices)
- ½ cup baby arugula

1. For bacon jam, cook bacon in large skillet over medium-high heat 10 to 15 minutes or until bacon is cooked through but still chewy (not crisp), stirring occasionally. Remove bacon to paper towel-lined plate. Drain off all but 1 tablespoon drippings from skillet.

2. Add onions to skillet; cook 10 minutes, stirring occasionally. Add brown sugar and red pepper flakes; cook over medium-low heat 18 to 20 minutes or until onions are deep golden brown. Stir in bacon, water and coffee; cook over medium heat 25 minutes or until mixture is thick and jammy, stirring occasionally. Stir in vinegar.*

3. For garlic aioli, combine mayonnaise, garlic, lemon juice and salt in small bowl; mix well.

4. Spread bottom halves of focaccia with garlic aioli. Top with tomatoes, cheese, turkey and arugula. Spread top halves of focaccia with bacon jam; place over arugula. Serve immediately.

Recipe makes about 1½ cups bacon jam. Store remaining jam in refrigerator up to 2 weeks; return to room temperature before serving.

SPICY CHICKEN SANDWICH

MAKES 4 SERVINGS

2 boneless skinless chicken breasts (about 8 ounces each)

1½ cups buttermilk

3 tablespoons hot pepper sauce, divided

1 teaspoon salt

⅓ cup mayonnaise

1 teaspoon Cajun seasoning

Canola or vegetable oil for frying

1 cup all-purpose flour

½ cup cornstarch

2 teaspoons paprika

1½ teaspoons black pepper

1 teaspoon msg

1 teaspoon ground red pepper

4 brioche sandwich buns, toasted and buttered

8 dill pickle slices

1. Pound chicken to ½-inch thickness between two sheets of waxed paper or plastic wrap. Cut each breast in half crosswise to create total of four pieces. Cut off pointed ends if necessary for more even rectangular shapes.

2. Combine buttermilk, 2 tablespoons hot pepper sauce and salt in medium bowl. Add chicken to brine; cover and refrigerate at least 4 hours or overnight. Combine mayonnaise, remaining 1 tablespoon hot pepper sauce and Cajun seasoning in small bowl; cover and refrigerate until ready to serve.

3. Remove chicken from refrigerator about 30 minutes before cooking. Heat at least 3 inches of oil in large saucepan over medium-high heat to 350°F; adjust heat to maintain temperature. Meanwhile, combine flour, cornstarch, paprika, black pepper, msg and red pepper in shallow dish; mix well. Drizzle 4 tablespoons buttermilk brine into flour mixture; stir with fork or fingers until mixture resembles wet sand.

4. Working with one piece at a time, remove chicken from brine and add to flour mixture. Turn to coat completely, pressing flour mixture into chicken to form thick coating. Lower chicken gently into hot oil; fry 6 to 8 minutes or until cooked through (165°F) and crust is golden brown and crisp, turning occasionally. Drain on paper towel-lined plate.

5. Spread about 1½ tablespoons mayonnaise mixture on cut sides of buns. Top bottom halves of buns with 2 pickle slices, chicken and top halves of buns. Serve immediately.

main dishes

INSPIRED BY CALIFORNIA PIZZA KITCHEN®

BARBECUE CHICKEN PIZZA

MAKES 4 SERVINGS

- 1 pound refrigerated pizza dough
- 1 tablespoon olive oil
- 6 ounces boneless skinless chicken breasts, cut into strips (about 2×¼ inch)
- ¼ teaspoon salt
- ⅛ teaspoon black pepper
- 6 tablespoons barbecue sauce, divided
- ⅔ cup shredded mozzarella cheese, divided
- ½ cup shredded smoked Gouda cheese, divided
- ½ small red onion, cut vertically into ⅛-inch slices
- 2 tablespoons chopped fresh cilantro

1. Preheat oven to 450°F. Line baking sheet with parchment paper. Let dough come to room temperature.

2. Heat oil in large skillet over medium-high heat. Season chicken with salt and pepper; cook about 5 minutes or just until cooked though, stirring occasionally. Remove chicken to medium bowl. Add 2 tablespoons barbecue sauce; stir to coat.

3. Roll out dough into 12-inch circle on lightly floured surface. Transfer to prepared baking sheet. Spread remaining 4 tablespoons barbecue sauce over dough, leaving ½-inch border. Sprinkle with 2 tablespoons mozzarella and 2 tablespoons Gouda cheese. Top with chicken and onion; sprinkle with remaining cheeses.

4. Bake 12 to 15 minutes or until crust is browned and cheese is bubbly. Sprinkle with cilantro.

FETTUCCINE ALFREDO

MAKES 4 SERVINGS

12 ounces uncooked fettuccine

⅔ cup whipping cream

6 tablespoons (¾ stick) butter

½ teaspoon salt

Generous dash white pepper

Generous dash ground nutmeg

1 cup grated Parmesan cheese

2 tablespoons chopped fresh Italian parsley

1. Cook pasta according to package directions. Drain well; cover and keep warm in saucepan.

2. Meanwhile, heat cream and butter in large heavy skillet over medium-low heat until butter melts and mixture bubbles, stirring frequently. Cook and stir 2 minutes. Stir in salt, pepper and nutmeg.

3. Remove from heat; gradually stir in Parmesan until well blended and smooth. Return to low heat, if necessary; do not let sauce bubble or cheese will become lumpy and tough.

4. Pour sauce over pasta; cook and stir over low heat 2 to 3 minutes or until sauce is thickened and pasta is evenly coated. Sprinkle with parsley. Serve immediately.

RESTAURANT-STYLE BABY BACK RIBS

MAKES 4 SERVINGS

1¼ cups water

1 cup white vinegar

⅔ cup packed dark brown sugar

½ cup tomato paste

1 tablespoon yellow mustard

1½ teaspoons salt

1 teaspoon liquid smoke

1 teaspoon onion powder

½ teaspoon garlic powder

½ teaspoon paprika

2 racks pork baby back ribs (3½ to 4 pounds total)

1. Combine water, vinegar, brown sugar, tomato paste, mustard, salt, liquid smoke, onion powder, garlic powder and paprika in medium saucepan; bring to a boil over medium heat. Reduce heat to medium-low; cook 40 minutes or until sauce thickens, stirring occasionally.

2. Preheat oven to 300°F. Place each rack of ribs on large sheet of heavy-duty foil. Brush some of sauce over ribs, covering completely. Fold down edges of foil tightly to seal and create packet; arrange packets on baking sheet, seam sides up.

3. Bake 2 hours. Prepare grill or preheat broiler. Carefully open packets and drain off excess liquid.

4. Brush ribs with sauce; grill or broil 5 minutes per side or until beginning to char, brushing with sauce once or twice during grilling. Serve with remaining sauce.

BOURBON-MARINATED SALMON

MAKES 4 SERVINGS

¼ cup packed brown sugar

¼ cup bourbon

¼ cup soy sauce

2 tablespoons lime juice

1 tablespoon grated fresh ginger

1 tablespoon minced garlic

¼ teaspoon black pepper

4 salmon fillets (7 to 8 ounces each)

2 tablespoons minced green onion

1. Combine brown sugar, bourbon, soy sauce, lime juice, ginger, garlic and pepper in medium bowl; mix well. Reserve ¼ cup mixture for serving; set aside.

2. Place salmon in large resealable food storage bag. Pour remaining marinade over salmon; seal bag and turn to coat. Marinate in refrigerator 2 to 4 hours, turning occasionally.

3. Prepare grill or preheat broiler. Remove salmon from marinade; discard marinade.

4. Grill or broil salmon 10 minutes or until fish begins to flake when tested with fork. (To broil, place salmon on foil-lined baking sheet sprayed with nonstick cooking spray.) Brush with reserved marinade mixture; sprinkle with green onion.

CHICKEN BURRITO BOWLS

MAKES 4 SERVINGS

- 3 cloves garlic
- ½ medium red onion, coarsely chopped
- 2 tablespoons olive oil
- 1½ tablespoons adobo sauce (from small can of chipotle peppers in adobo)
- 1 tablespoon ancho chili powder
- 1½ teaspoons ground cumin
- 1 teaspoon salt
- 1 teaspoon dried oregano
- ½ teaspoon black pepper
- ½ cup water
- 1 pound boneless skinless chicken thighs
- 1⅓ cups cooked black beans
- 3 cups cooked white or brown rice

  Optional toppings: guacamole, salsa, corn, shredded lettuce, shredded Monterey Jack cheese, lime wedges and sour cream

1. With motor running, drop garlic cloves through feed tube of food processor; process until garlic is finely chopped. Add onion, oil, adobo sauce, chili powder, cumin, salt, oregano and pepper; process until well blended. Add water; process until smooth.

2. Place chicken in large resealable food storage bag. Add marinade; seal bag and turn to coat. Refrigerate at least 3 hours or overnight.

3. Remove chicken from refrigerator about 30 minutes before cooking. Prepare grill for direct cooking or preheat grill pan.* Grill chicken about 6 minutes per side or until cooked through (165°F). Remove to large plate; tent with foil. Let stand 10 minutes before chopping into ½-inch pieces.

4. Serve chicken and beans over rice with desired toppings.

Or cook chicken in large skillet in 1 tablespoon olive oil over medium-high heat about 6 minutes per side or until browned and cooked through.

MONGOLIAN BEEF

MAKES 4 SERVINGS

1¼ pounds beef flank steak

¼ cup cornstarch

3 tablespoons vegetable oil, divided

3 cloves garlic, minced

2 teaspoons grated fresh ginger

½ cup water

½ cup soy sauce

⅓ cup packed dark brown sugar

Pinch red pepper flakes

2 green onions, diagonally sliced into 1-inch pieces

Hot cooked rice (optional)

1. Cut flank steak in half lengthwise, then cut crosswise (against the grain) into ¼-inch slices. Combine beef and cornstarch in medium bowl; toss to coat.

2. Heat 1 tablespoon oil in large skillet or wok over high heat. Add half of beef in single layer (do not crowd); cook 1 to 2 minutes per side or until browned. Remove to clean bowl. Repeat with remaining beef and 1 tablespoon oil.

3. Heat remaining 1 tablespoon oil in same skillet over medium heat. Add garlic and ginger; cook and stir 30 seconds. Add water, soy sauce, brown sugar and red pepper flakes; bring to a boil, stirring until well blended. Cook about 8 minutes or until slightly thickened, stirring occasionally.

4. Return beef to skillet; cook 2 to 3 minutes or until sauce thickens and beef is heated through. Stir in green onions. Serve with rice, if desired.

EGGPLANT PARMESAN

MAKES 4 SERVINGS

- 2 tablespoons olive oil
- 2 cloves garlic, minced
- 1 can (28 ounces) Italian whole tomatoes, undrained
- ½ cup water
- 1¼ teaspoons salt, divided
- ¼ teaspoon dried oregano
- Pinch red pepper flakes
- 1 medium eggplant (about 1 pound)
- ⅓ cup all-purpose flour
- Black pepper
- ⅔ cup milk
- 1 egg
- 1 cup Italian-seasoned dry bread crumbs
- 4 to 5 tablespoons vegetable oil, divided
- 1 cup (4 ounces) shredded mozzarella cheese
- Chopped fresh parsley (optional)

1. Heat olive oil in medium saucepan over medium heat. Add garlic; cook and stir 2 minutes or until softened (do not brown). Crush tomatoes with hands (in bowl or in can); add to saucepan with juices from can. Stir in water, 1 teaspoon salt, oregano and red pepper flakes; bring to a simmer. Reduce heat to medium-low; cook 45 minutes, stirring occasionally.

2. Meanwhile, prepare eggplant. Cut eggplant crosswise into ¼-inch slices. Combine flour, remaining ¼ teaspoon salt and black pepper in shallow dish. Beat milk and egg in another shallow dish. Place bread crumbs in third shallow dish.

3. Coat both sides of eggplant slices with flour mixture, shaking off excess. Dip in egg mixture, letting excess drip back into dish. Roll in bread crumbs to coat.

4. Heat 3 tablespoons vegetable oil in large skillet over medium-high heat. Working in batches, add eggplant slices to skillet in single layer; cook 3 to 4 minutes per side or until golden brown, adding additional vegetable oil as needed. Remove to paper towel-lined plate; cover loosely with foil to keep warm.

5. Preheat broiler. Spray 13×9-inch baking dish with nonstick cooking spray. Arrange eggplant slices overlapping in baking dish; top with half of warm marinara sauce. (Reserve remaining marinara sauce for pasta or another use.) Sprinkle with cheese.

6. Broil 2 to 3 minutes or just until cheese is melted and beginning to brown. Garnish with parsley.

PERI-PERI CHICKEN

MAKES 4 SERVINGS

INSPIRED BY NANDO'S® PERI-PERI CHICKEN

- 1 small red onion, coarsely chopped
- 1 roasted red pepper (about 3 ounces)
- ¼ cup olive oil
- ¼ cup lemon juice
- 2 tablespoons white vinegar
- 4 cloves garlic, minced
- 1 tablespoon smoked paprika
- 1½ teaspoons salt
- 1½ teaspoons red pepper flakes
- 1 teaspoon dried oregano
- ½ teaspoon black pepper
- 1 cut-up whole chicken (3 to 4 pounds)

1. Combine onion, roasted pepper, oil, lemon juice, vinegar, garlic, smoked paprika, salt, red pepper flakes, oregano and black pepper in blender or food processor; blend until smooth. Remove half of marinade to small bowl; cover and refrigerate until ready to use.

2. Use sharp knife to make several slashes in each piece of chicken (about ¼ inch deep). Place chicken in large resealable food storage bag. Pour remaining marinade over chicken; seal bag and turn to coat, massaging marinade into chicken. Marinate chicken in refrigerator at least 4 hours or overnight, turning occasionally.

3. Remove chicken from refrigerator about 30 minutes before cooking. Preheat oven to 400°F.* Line baking sheet with foil. Arrange chicken on baking sheet.

4. Bake about 45 minutes or until chicken is cooked through (165°F), brushing with some of reserved marinade every 15 minutes. Serve with remaining marinade, if desired.

*For a smokier flavor, grill chicken over medium heat 30 to 40 minutes or until cooked through (165°F).

MEATBALLS AND RICOTTA

MAKES 5 TO 6 SERVINGS

MEATBALLS

- 2 tablespoons olive oil
- ½ cup plain dry bread crumbs
- ½ cup milk
- 1 cup finely chopped yellow onion
- 2 green onions, finely chopped
- ½ cup grated Romano cheese, plus additional for serving
- 2 eggs, beaten
- ¼ cup finely chopped fresh parsley
- ¼ cup finely chopped fresh basil
- 2 cloves garlic, minced
- 2 teaspoons salt
- ¼ teaspoon black pepper
- 1 pound ground beef
- 1 pound ground pork

SAUCE

- 2 tablespoons olive oil
- 2 tablespoons butter
- 1 cup finely chopped yellow onion
- 1 clove garlic, minced
- 1 can (28 ounces) whole Italian plum tomatoes, undrained, coarsely chopped
- 1 can (28 ounces) crushed tomatoes

- 1 teaspoon salt
- ¼ teaspoon black pepper
- ¼ cup finely chopped fresh basil
- 1 to 1½ cups ricotta cheese

1. Preheat oven to 375°F. Brush 2 tablespoons oil over large rimmed baking sheet.

2. Combine bread crumbs and milk in large bowl; mix well. Add 1 cup yellow onion, green onions, ½ cup Romano, eggs, parsley, ¼ cup basil, 2 cloves garlic, 2 teaspoons salt and ¼ teaspoon black pepper; mix well. Add beef and pork; mix gently but thoroughly until blended. Shape mixture by ¼ cupfuls into balls. Place meatballs on prepared baking sheet; turn to coat with oil.

3. Bake about 20 minutes or until meatballs are cooked through (160°F). Meanwhile, prepare sauce.

4. Heat 2 tablespoons oil and butter in large saucepan over medium heat until butter is melted. Add 1 cup yellow onion; cook 8 minutes or until tender and lightly browned, stirring frequently. Add 1 clove garlic; cook and stir 1 minute or until fragrant. Add plum tomatoes with juice, crushed tomatoes, 1 teaspoon salt and ¼ teaspoon black pepper; bring to a simmer. Reduce heat to medium-low; cook 20 minutes, stirring occasionally.

5. Stir ¼ cup basil into sauce. Add meatballs; cook 10 minutes, stirring occasionally. Transfer meatballs and sauce to serving dish; dollop tablespoonfuls of ricotta between meatballs. Garnish with additional Romano.

ISLAND FISH TACOS

MAKES 4 SERVINGS

COLESLAW

- 1 medium jicama (about 12 ounces), peeled and shredded
- 2 cups packaged coleslaw mix
- 3 tablespoons finely chopped fresh cilantro
- ¼ cup lime juice
- ¼ cup vegetable oil
- 3 tablespoons white vinegar
- 2 tablespoons mayonnaise
- 1 tablespoon honey
- 1 teaspoon salt

SALSA

- 2 medium fresh tomatoes, diced (about 2 cups)
- ½ cup finely chopped red onion
- ¼ cup finely chopped fresh cilantro
- 2 tablespoons lime juice
- 2 tablespoons minced jalapeño pepper
- 1 teaspoon salt

TACOS

- 1 to 1¼ pounds white fish such as tilapia or mahi mahi, cut into 3×1½-inch pieces
- Salt and black pepper
- 2 tablespoons vegetable oil
- 12 (6-inch) taco-size tortillas, heated
- Prepared guacamole (optional)

1. For coleslaw, combine jicama, coleslaw mix and 3 tablespoons cilantro in medium bowl. Whisk ¼ cup lime juice, ¼ cup oil, vinegar, mayonnaise, honey and 1 teaspoon salt in small bowl until well blended. Pour over vegetable mixture; stir to coat. Let stand at least 15 minutes for flavors to blend.

2. For salsa, place tomatoes in fine-mesh strainer; set in bowl or sink to drain 15 minutes. Transfer to another medium bowl. Stir in onion, ¼ cup cilantro, 2 tablespoons lime juice, jalapeño pepper and 1 teaspoon salt; mix well.

3. For tacos, season both sides of fish with salt and black pepper. Heat 1 tablespoon oil in large nonstick skillet over medium-high heat. Add half of fish; cook about 2 minutes per side or until fish is opaque and begins to flake when tested with fork. Repeat with remaining oil and fish.

4. Break fish into bite-size pieces; serve in tortillas with coleslaw, salsa and guacamole, if desired.

BANGKOK PEANUT NOODLES

MAKES 4 SERVINGS

SAUCE

- 6 tablespoons peanut butter
- ¼ cup soy sauce
- 1 tablespoon unseasoned rice vinegar
- 1 tablespoon packed brown sugar
- 1 tablespoon sriracha sauce
- 2 teaspoons grated fresh ginger
- 2 cloves garlic, minced
- 2 teaspoons dark sesame oil

STIR-FRY

- 1 package (6 ounces) dried chow mein stir-fry noodles
- 1 pound boneless skinless chicken breasts, cut into 1-inch pieces *or* 1 package (14 ounces) extra firm tofu, cut into ½-inch cubes
- ½ cup cornstarch
- 3 tablespoons vegetable oil, divided
- 1 red bell pepper, cut into thin strips
- ½ medium onion, thinly sliced
- 2 cups sliced Swiss chard or bok choy

1. For sauce, whisk peanut butter, soy sauce, vinegar, brown sugar, sriracha, ginger, garlic and sesame oil in small bowl until smooth.

2. For stir-fry, cook noodles according to package directions; drain and rinse under cold water until cool.

3. Combine chicken and cornstarch in medium bowl; toss to coat. Heat 2 tablespoons vegetable oil in large skillet over medium-high heat. Add chicken; stir-fry 5 minutes or until chicken is golden brown and cooked through. Drain on paper towel-lined plate. Wipe out skillet with paper towel.

4. Heat remaining 1 tablespoon vegetable oil in same skillet over high heat. Add bell pepper and onion; stir-fry 5 minutes or until browned. Add chard; stir-fry 1 minute or until wilted. Add noodles and sauce; cook and stir until noodles are coated with sauce. Add 1 tablespoon water if needed to loosen sauce. Return chicken to skillet; stir to coat. Cook just until heated through.

MEATLOAF

MAKES 6 TO 8 SERVINGS

- 1 tablespoon vegetable oil
- 2 green onions, minced
- ¼ cup minced green bell pepper
- ¼ cup grated carrot
- 3 cloves garlic, minced
- ¾ cup milk
- 2 eggs, beaten
- 1 pound ground beef
- 1 pound ground pork
- 1 cup plain dry bread crumbs
- 2 teaspoons salt
- ½ teaspoon onion powder
- ½ teaspoon black pepper
- ½ cup ketchup, divided

1. Preheat oven to 350°F.

2. Heat oil in large skillet over medium-high heat. Add green onions, bell pepper, carrot and garlic; cook and stir 5 minutes or until vegetables are softened.

3. Whisk milk and eggs in medium bowl until well blended. Gently mix beef, pork, bread crumbs, salt, onion powder and black pepper in large bowl with hands. Add milk mixture, vegetables and ¼ cup ketchup; mix gently. Press into 9×5-inch loaf pan; place pan on rimmed baking sheet.

4. Bake 30 minutes. Spread remaining ¼ cup ketchup over meatloaf; bake 1 hour or until cooked through (160°F). Cool in pan 10 minutes; cut into slices.

CLASSIC LASAGNA

MAKES 6 TO 8 SERVINGS

- 1 tablespoon olive oil
- 8 ounces bulk mild Italian sausage
- 8 ounces ground beef
- 1 medium onion, chopped
- 3 cloves garlic, minced, divided
- 1½ teaspoons salt, divided
- 1 can (28 ounces) crushed tomatoes
- 1 can (28 ounces) diced tomatoes
- 2 teaspoons Italian seasoning
- 1 egg
- 1 container (15 ounces) ricotta cheese
- ¾ cup grated Parmesan cheese, divided
- ½ cup minced fresh parsley
- ¼ teaspoon black pepper
- 12 uncooked no-boil lasagna noodles
- 4 cups (16 ounces) shredded mozzarella

1. Preheat oven to 350°F. Spray 13×9-inch baking dish with nonstick cooking spray.

2. Heat oil in large saucepan over medium-high heat. Add sausage, beef, onion, 2 cloves garlic and 1 teaspoon salt; cook and stir 10 minutes or until meat is no longer pink, breaking up meat with wooden spoon. Add crushed tomatoes, diced tomatoes and Italian seasoning; bring to a boil. Reduce heat to medium-low; cook 15 minutes, stirring occasionally.

3. Meanwhile, beat egg in medium bowl. Stir in ricotta, ½ cup Parmesan, parsley, remaining 1 clove garlic, ½ teaspoon salt and pepper until well blended.

4. Spread ¼ cup sauce in prepared baking dish. Top with 3 noodles, breaking to fit if necessary. Spread one third of ricotta mixture over noodles. Sprinkle with 1 cup mozzarella; top with 2 cups sauce. Repeat layers of noodles, ricotta mixture, mozzarella and sauce two times. Top with remaining 3 noodles, sauce, 1 cup mozzarella and ¼ cup Parmesan. Cover dish with foil sprayed with cooking spray.

5. Bake 30 minutes. Remove foil; bake 10 to 15 minutes or until hot and bubbly. Let stand 10 minutes before serving.

STEAK FAJITAS

MAKES 2 SERVINGS

¼ cup lime juice

¼ cup soy sauce

4 tablespoons vegetable oil, divided

2 tablespoons honey

2 tablespoons Worcestershire sauce

2 cloves garlic, minced

½ teaspoon ground red pepper

1 pound flank steak, skirt steak or top sirloin

1 medium yellow onion, halved and cut into ¼-inch slices

1 green bell pepper, cut into ¼-inch strips

1 red bell pepper, cut into ¼-inch strips

Flour tortillas, warmed

Lime wedges (optional)

Optional toppings: pico de gallo, guacamole, sour cream, shredded lettuce and shredded Cheddar-Jack cheese

1. Combine lime juice, soy sauce, 2 tablespoons oil, honey, Worcestershire sauce, garlic and ground red pepper in medium bowl; mix well. Remove ¼ cup marinade to large bowl. Place steak in large resealable food storage bag. Pour remaining marinade over steak; seal bag and turn to coat. Marinate in refrigerator at least 2 hours or overnight. Add onion and bell peppers to bowl with ¼ cup marinade; toss to coat. Cover and refrigerate until ready to use.

2. Remove steak from marinade; discard marinade and pat steak dry with paper towels. Heat 1 tablespoon oil in large skillet (preferably cast iron) over medium-high heat. Cook steak about 4 minutes per side for medium rare or to desired doneness. Remove to cutting board; tent with foil and let stand 10 minutes.

3. Meanwhile, heat remaining 1 tablespoon oil in same skillet over medium-high heat. Add vegetable mixture; cook about 8 minutes or until vegetables are crisp-tender and beginning to brown in spots, stirring occasionally. (Cook in two batches if necessary; do not crowd vegetables in skillet.)

4. Cut steak into thin slices across the grain. Serve with vegetables, tortillas, lime wedges and desired toppings.

CHICKEN MARSALA

MAKES 4 SERVINGS

- 4 boneless skinless chicken breasts (6 to 8 ounces each)
- ½ cup all-purpose flour
- 1 teaspoon coarse salt
- ¼ teaspoon black pepper
- 2 tablespoons olive oil
- 3 tablespoons butter, divided
- 2 cups (16 ounces) sliced mushrooms
- 1 shallot, minced (about 2 tablespoons)
- 1 clove garlic, minced
- 1 cup dry Marsala wine
- ½ cup chicken broth
  Finely chopped fresh parsley

1. Pound chicken to ¼-inch thickness between two sheets of plastic wrap. Combine flour, salt and pepper in shallow dish; mix well. Coat both sides of chicken with flour mixture, shaking off excess.

2. Heat oil and 1 tablespoon butter in large skillet over medium-high heat. Add chicken in single layer; cook about 4 minutes per side or until golden brown. Remove to plate; cover loosely with foil to keep warm.

3. Add 1 tablespoon butter, mushrooms and shallot to skillet; cook about 10 minutes or until mushrooms are deep golden brown, stirring occasionally. Add garlic; cook and stir 1 minute. Stir in wine and broth; cook 2 minutes, scraping up browned bits from bottom of skillet. Stir in remaining 1 tablespoon butter until melted.

4. Return chicken to skillet; turn to coat with sauce. Cook 2 minutes or until heated through. Sprinkle with parsley.

PASTA CAMPAGNOLO

MAKES 4 SERVINGS

- 3 tablespoons olive oil
- 8 ounces Italian sausage, casings removed
- 1 small onion, finely chopped
- 1 red bell pepper, cut into ¼-inch strips
- 2 cloves garlic, minced
- ⅓ cup dry white wine
- 1 can (28 ounces) crushed tomatoes
- 1 can (8 ounces) tomato sauce
- 4 tablespoons chopped fresh basil, divided, plus additional for garnish
- ½ teaspoon salt
- ¼ teaspoon black pepper
- ⅛ teaspoon red pepper flakes
- 1 package (16 ounces) uncooked rigatoni or penne pasta
- ¼ cup grated Romano cheese
- 1 package (4 ounces) goat cheese, cut crosswise into 8 slices

1. Heat oil in large saucepan over medium heat. Break sausage into ½-inch pieces; add to saucepan. Cook about 5 minutes or until browned, stirring occasionally. Add onion and bell pepper; cook and stir 4 minutes or until vegetables are softened. Add garlic; cook and stir 1 minute.

2. Stir in wine; cook about 5 minutes or until most of liquid has evaporated. Stir in tomatoes, tomato sauce, 2 tablespoons basil, salt, black pepper and red pepper flakes; bring to a boil. Reduce heat to medium-low; cook 20 minutes or until sauce has thickened slightly.

3. Meanwhile, cook pasta in boiling salted water according to package directions until al dente. Add hot cooked pasta, Romano cheese and remaining 2 tablespoons basil to sauce; stir gently to coat. Cook just until heated through.

4. Top each serving with 1 or 2 slices of goat cheese; garnish with additional basil.

COCONUT SHRIMP

MAKES 4 SERVINGS

DIPPING SAUCE

- ½ cup orange marmalade
- ⅓ cup Thai chili sauce
- 1 teaspoon prepared horseradish
- ½ teaspoon salt

SHRIMP

- 1 cup flat beer
- 1 cup all-purpose flour
- 2 cups sweetened flaked coconut, divided
- 2 tablespoons sugar
    Vegetable oil for frying
- 16 to 20 large raw shrimp, peeled and deveined (with tails on), patted dry

1. For sauce, combine marmalade, chili sauce, horseradish and salt in small bowl; mix well. Cover and refrigerate until ready to serve.

2. For shrimp, whisk beer, flour, ½ cup coconut and sugar in large bowl until well blended. Refrigerate batter until oil is hot. Place remaining 1½ cups coconut in medium bowl.

3. Heat 2 inches of oil in large saucepan over medium heat to 350°F; adjust heat to maintain temperature. Dip each shrimp in beer batter, then in coconut, turning to coat completely. Fry shrimp, four at a time, 2 to 3 minutes or until golden brown, turning halfway through cooking time. Drain on paper towel-lined plate. Serve immediately with dipping sauce.

FRENCH QUARTER STEAKS

MAKES 2 SERVINGS

- ½ cup water
- 2 tablespoons Worcestershire sauce
- 2 tablespoons soy sauce
- 1 tablespoon chili powder
- 3 cloves garlic, minced, divided
- 2 teaspoons paprika
- 1½ teaspoons ground red pepper
- 1¼ teaspoons black pepper, divided
- 1 teaspoon onion powder
- 2 top sirloin steaks (about 8 ounces each, 1 inch thick)
- 3 tablespoons butter, divided
- 1 tablespoon olive oil
- 1 large onion, thinly sliced
- 8 ounces sliced mushrooms (white and shiitake or all white)
- ¼ teaspoon plus ⅛ teaspoon salt, divided

1. Combine water, Worcestershire sauce, soy sauce, chili powder, 2 cloves garlic, paprika, red pepper, 1 teaspoon black pepper and onion powder in small bowl; mix well. Place steaks in large resealable food storage bag; pour marinade over steaks. Seal bag; turn to coat. Marinate in refrigerator 1 to 3 hours.

2. Remove steaks from marinade 30 minutes before cooking; discard marinade and pat steaks dry with paper towel. Prepare grill for direct cooking. Oil grid.

3. While grill is preheating, heat 1 tablespoon butter and oil in large skillet over medium high heat. Add onion; cook 5 minutes, stirring occasionally. Add mushrooms, ¼ teaspoon salt and remaining ¼ teaspoon black pepper; cook 10 minutes or until onion is golden brown and mushrooms are beginning to brown, stirring occasionally. Combine remaining 2 tablespoons butter, 1 clove garlic and ⅛ teaspoon salt in small skillet; cook over medium-low heat 3 minutes or until garlic begins to sizzle.

4. Grill steaks over medium-high heat 6 minutes; turn and cook 6 minutes for medium rare or until desired doneness. Brush both sides of steaks with garlic butter during last 2 minutes of cooking. Remove to plate and tent with foil; let rest 5 minutes. Serve steaks with onion and mushroom mixture.

PESTO CAVATAPPI

MAKES 4 TO 6 SERVINGS

PESTO

- 2 cups packed fresh basil leaves*
- 1 cup walnuts, toasted**
- ½ cup shredded Parmesan cheese, plus additional for garnish
- 4 cloves garlic
- 1 teaspoon salt
- ¼ teaspoon black pepper
- ¾ cup extra virgin olive oil

PASTA

- 1 package (16 ounces) uncooked cavatappi pasta
- 1 tablespoon extra virgin olive oil
- 2 plum tomatoes, diced (1½ cups)
- 1 package (8 ounces) sliced mushrooms
- ¼ cup dry white wine
- ¼ cup vegetable broth
- ¼ cup whipping cream

Or substitute 1 cup packed fresh parsley leaves for half of basil.

**To toast walnuts, cook in medium skillet over medium heat 4 to 5 minutes or lightly browned, stirring frequently.*

1. For pesto, combine basil, walnuts, ½ cup cheese, garlic, salt and black pepper in food processor; pulse until coarsely chopped. With motor running, add ¾ cup oil in thin, steady stream; process until well blended. Measure 1 cup pesto for pasta; reserve remaining pesto for another use.

2. Cook pasta in large saucepan of boiling salted water according to package directions until al dente. Drain and return to saucepan; keep warm.

3. Meanwhile, heat 1 tablespoon oil in large skillet over medium-high heat. Add tomatoes and mushrooms; cook about 7 minutes or until most of liquid has evaporated, stirring occasionally. Add wine, broth and cream; bring to a boil. Reduce heat to low; cook about 4 minutes or until sauce has thickened slightly. Stir in 1 cup pesto; cook just until heated through.

4. Pour sauce over pasta; stir gently to coat. Divide pasta among serving bowls; garnish with additional cheese.

AUSSIE CHICKEN

MAKES 4 SERVINGS

½ cup honey

½ cup Dijon mustard

2 tablespoons vegetable oil, divided

1 teaspoon lemon juice

4 boneless skinless chicken breasts (about 6 ounces each)

   Salt and black pepper

1 tablespoon butter

2 cups sliced mushrooms

4 slices bacon, cooked

½ cup (2 ounces) shredded Cheddar cheese

½ cup (2 ounces) shredded Monterey Jack cheese

   Chopped fresh parsley

1. Whisk honey, mustard, 1 tablespoon oil and lemon juice in medium bowl until well blended. Reserve half of marinade mixture to use as sauce; cover and refrigerate until ready to serve.

2. Place chicken in large resealable food storage bag. Pour remaining half of marinade over chicken; seal bag and turn to coat. Refrigerate at least 2 hours.

3. Preheat oven to 375°F. Remove chicken from marinade; discard marinade. Heat remaining 1 tablespoon oil in large ovenproof skillet over medium-high heat. Add chicken; cook 3 to 4 minutes per side or until golden brown. (Chicken will not be cooked through.) Remove to plate; sprinkle with salt and pepper.

4. Heat butter in same skillet over medium-high heat. Add mushrooms; cook 8 minutes or until mushrooms begin to brown, stirring occasionally and scraping up browned bits from bottom of skillet. Season with salt and pepper. Return chicken to skillet; spoon mushrooms over chicken. Top with bacon; sprinkle with Cheddar and Monterey Jack cheeses.

5. Bake 8 to 10 minutes or until chicken is cooked through (165°F) and cheeses are melted. Sprinkle with parsley; serve with reserved honey-mustard mixture.

JAMBALAYA PASTA

MAKES 4 SERVINGS

1 pound boneless skinless chicken breasts, cut into 1-inch pieces

2 tablespoons plus 1 teaspoon Cajun seasoning, divided

1 tablespoon vegetable oil

8 ounces bell peppers (red, yellow, green or a combination), cut into ¼-inch strips

½ medium red onion, cut into ¼-inch strips

6 ounces medium raw shrimp, peeled and deveined

2 cloves garlic, minced

1 teaspoon salt

¼ teaspoon black pepper

1½ pounds plum tomatoes (about 6), cut into ½-inch pieces

1 cup chicken broth

1 package (16 ounces) fresh or dried linguini, cooked and drained

Chopped fresh parsley

1. Combine chicken and 2 tablespoons Cajun seasoning in medium bowl; toss to coat. Heat oil in large skillet over medium-high heat. Add chicken; cook and stir 3 minutes.

2. Add bell peppers and onion; cook and stir 3 minutes. Add shrimp, garlic, remaining 1 teaspoon Cajun seasoning, salt and black pepper; cook and stir 1 minute.

3. Stir in tomatoes and broth; bring to a boil. Reduce heat to medium-low; cook 3 minutes or until shrimp are pink and opaque. Serve over hot pasta; sprinkle with parsley.

side dishes

INSPIRED BY
KFC®

COLESLAW

MAKES 10 SERVINGS

- 1 medium head green cabbage, shredded
- 1 medium carrot, shredded
- ½ cup mayonnaise
- ½ cup milk
- ⅓ cup sugar
- 3 tablespoons lemon juice
- 1½ tablespoons white vinegar
- ½ teaspoon salt
- ⅛ teaspoon black pepper

1. Combine cabbage and carrot in large bowl; mix well.

2. Combine mayonnaise, milk, sugar, lemon juice, vinegar, salt and pepper in medium bowl; whisk until well blended. Add to cabbage mixture; stir until blended.

SOFT GARLIC BREADSTICKS

MAKES ABOUT 16 BREADSTICKS

1½ cups water

6 tablespoons (¾ stick) butter, divided

4 cups all-purpose flour

2 tablespoons sugar

1 package (¼ ounce) active dry yeast

1½ teaspoons salt

¾ teaspoon coarse salt

¼ teaspoon garlic powder

1. Heat water and 2 tablespoons butter in small saucepan or microwavable bowl to 110° to 115°F. (Butter does not need to melt completely.)

2. Combine flour, sugar, yeast and 1½ teaspoons salt in large bowl of stand mixer. Add water mixture; knead with dough hook at low speed until dough begins to come together. Mix about 5 minutes or until dough is smooth and elastic. Shape dough into a ball. Place in large greased bowl; turn to grease top. Cover and let rise in warm place about 1 hour or until doubled in size.

3. Line two baking sheets with parchment paper or spray with nonstick cooking spray. Punch down dough. For each breadstick, pull off piece of dough slightly larger than a golf ball (about 2 ounces) and roll between hands or on work surface into 7-inch-long rope. Place on prepared baking sheets; cover loosely and let rise in warm place about 45 minutes or until doubled in size.

4. Preheat oven to 400°F. Melt remaining 4 tablespoons butter. Brush breadsticks with 2 tablespoons butter; sprinkle with coarse salt.

5. Bake breadsticks 13 to 15 minutes or until golden brown. Stir garlic powder into remaining 2 tablespoons melted butter; brush over breadsticks immediately after removing from oven. Serve warm.

LOADED BAKED POTATOES

MAKES 4 SERVINGS

- 4 large baking potatoes
- 1 cup (4 ounces) shredded Cheddar cheese
- 1 cup (4 ounces) shredded Monterey Jack cheese
- 8 slices bacon, crisp-cooked
- ½ cup sour cream
- ¼ cup (½ stick) butter, melted
- 2 tablespoons milk
- 1 teaspoon salt
- ¼ teaspoon black pepper
- 1 tablespoon vegetable oil
- 2 teaspoons coarse salt
- 1 green onion, thinly sliced (optional)

1. Preheat oven to 400°F. Prick potatoes all over with fork; place in small baking pan. Bake about 1 hour or until potatoes are fork-tender. Let stand until cool enough to handle. *Reduce oven temperature to 350°F.*

2. Combine Cheddar and Monterey Jack cheeses in small bowl; reserve ¼ cup for garnish. Chop bacon; reserve ¼ cup for garnish.

3. Cut off thin slice from one long side of each potato. Scoop out centers of potatoes, leaving ¼-inch shell. Place flesh from 3 potatoes in medium bowl. (Reserve flesh from fourth potato for another use.) Add sour cream, butter, remaining 1¾ cups shredded cheese, bacon, milk, 1 teaspoon salt and pepper to bowl with potatoes; mash until well blended.

4. Turn potato shells over; brush bottoms and sides with oil. Sprinkle evenly with coarse salt. Turn right side up and return to baking pan. Fill shells with mashed potato mixture, mounding over tops of shells. Sprinkle with reserved cheese and bacon.

5. Bake about 20 minutes or until filling is hot and cheese is melted. Garnish with green onion.

STEAKHOUSE CREAMED SPINACH

MAKES 4 SERVINGS

- 1 **pound baby spinach**
- ½ **cup (1 stick) butter**
- 2 **tablespoons finely chopped onion**
- ¼ **cup all-purpose flour**
- 2 **cups whole milk**
- 1 **bay leaf**
- ½ **teaspoon salt**
  Pinch ground nutmeg
  Pinch ground red pepper
  Black pepper

1. Heat medium saucepan of water to a boil over high heat. Add spinach; cook 1 minute. Drain and remove to bowl of ice water to stop cooking. Squeeze spinach dry; coarsely chop. Wipe out saucepan with paper towel.

2. Melt butter in same saucepan over medium heat. Add onion; cook and stir 2 minutes or until softened. Add flour; cook and stir 2 to 3 minutes or until slightly golden. Slowly add milk in thin, steady stream, whisking constantly until mixture boils and begins to thicken. Stir in bay leaf, ½ teaspoon salt, nutmeg and red pepper. Reduce heat to low; cook and stir 5 minutes. Remove and discard bay leaf.

3. Stir in spinach; cook 5 minutes, stirring frequently. Season with additional salt and black pepper.

JALAPEÑO BEANS

MAKES 4 TO 6 SERVINGS

- 1 tablespoon vegetable oil
- 1 small onion, finely chopped
- 1 teaspoon ground cumin
- 1 teaspoon garlic powder
- ½ teaspoon smoked paprika
- ¼ teaspoon ground red pepper
- 3 tablespoons chopped pickled jalapeño peppers
- 2 cans (about 15 ounces each) chili beans (made with pinto beans)
- ⅓ cup dark lager beer
- 1 tablespoon white vinegar
- 1 teaspoon sugar
- ½ teaspoon hot pepper sauce

  Salt and black pepper

1. Heat oil in large saucepan over medium-high heat. Add onion; cook and stir 2 minutes or until translucent. Add cumin, garlic powder, paprika and red pepper; cook and stir 1 minute. Add pickled jalapeños; cook and stir 30 seconds.

2. Stir in beans, beer, vinegar, sugar and hot pepper sauce; bring to a boil. Reduce heat to medium-low; cook 15 minutes, stirring occasionally. Season with salt and black pepper. Beans will thicken upon standing.

CHEDDAR BISCUITS

MAKES 15 BISCUITS

- 2 cups all-purpose flour
- 1 tablespoon sugar
- 1 tablespoon baking powder
- 2¼ teaspoons garlic powder, divided
- ¾ teaspoon plus pinch of salt, divided
- 1 cup whole milk
- ½ cup (1 stick) plus 3 tablespoons butter, melted, divided
- 2 cups (8 ounces) shredded Cheddar cheese
- ½ teaspoon dried parsley flakes

1. Preheat oven to 450°F. Line baking sheet with parchment paper.

2. Combine flour, sugar, baking powder, 2 teaspoons garlic powder and ¾ teaspoon salt in large bowl; mix well. Add milk and ½ cup melted butter; stir just until dry ingredients are moistened. Stir in cheese just until blended. Drop scant ¼ cupfuls of dough about 1½ inches apart onto prepared baking sheet.

3. Bake 10 to 12 minutes or until golden brown.

4. Meanwhile, combine remaining 3 tablespoons melted butter, ¼ teaspoon garlic powder, pinch of salt and parsley flakes in small bowl; brush over biscuits immediately after removing from oven. Serve warm.

SMASHED POTATOES

MAKES 4 SERVINGS

4 medium russet potatoes (about 1½ pounds), peeled and cut into ¼-inch cubes

⅓ cup milk

2 tablespoons sour cream

1 tablespoon minced onion

½ teaspoon salt

¼ teaspoon black pepper

⅛ teaspoon garlic powder (optional)

Chopped fresh chives or French fried onions (optional)

1. Bring large saucepan of lightly salted water to a boil over medium-high heat. Add potatoes; cook 15 to 20 minutes or until fork-tender. Drain and return to saucepan.

2. Slightly mash potatoes. Stir in milk, sour cream, minced onion, salt, pepper and garlic powder, if desired. Mash until desired texture is reached, leaving potatoes chunky.

3. Cook 5 minutes over low heat or until heated through, stirring occasionally. Top with chives, if desired.

232

side dishes

SIMPLE GOLDEN CORN BREAD

MAKES 9 TO 12 SERVINGS

1¼ cups all-purpose flour
¾ cup yellow cornmeal
⅓ cup sugar
2 teaspoons baking powder
1 teaspoon salt
1¼ cups whole milk
¼ cup (½ stick) butter, melted
1 egg
   Honey Butter (recipe
      follows, optional)

1. Preheat oven to 400°F. Spray 8-inch square baking dish or pan with nonstick cooking spray.

2. Combine flour, cornmeal, sugar, baking powder and salt in large bowl; mix well. Beat milk, butter and egg in medium bowl until well blended. Add to flour mixture; stir just until dry ingredients are moistened. Pour batter into prepared baking dish.

3. Bake 25 minutes or until golden brown and toothpick inserted into center comes out clean. Prepare Honey Butter, if desired. Serve with corn bread.

/////////////////////////////////

honey butter

Beat 6 tablespoons (¾ stick) softened butter and ¼ cup honey in medium bowl with electric mixer at medium-high speed until light and creamy.

CLASSIC MACARONI AND CHEESE

MAKES 8 SERVINGS

side dishes

- 2 cups uncooked elbow macaroni
- ¼ cup (½ stick) butter
- ¼ cup all-purpose flour
- 2½ cups whole milk
- 1 teaspoon salt
- ⅛ teaspoon black pepper
- 4 cups (16 ounces) shredded Colby-Jack cheese

1. Cook pasta according to package directions until al dente; drain.

2. Melt butter in large saucepan over medium heat. Add flour; whisk until well blended and bubbly. Slowly add milk, salt and pepper, whisking until blended. Cook and stir until milk begins to bubble. Add cheese, 1 cup at a time; cook and stir until cheese is melted and sauce is smooth.

3. Add cooked pasta to saucepan; stir gently until blended. Cook until heated through.

HUSH PUPPIES

MAKES ABOUT 24 HUSH PUPPIES

side dishes

1½ cups yellow cornmeal
½ cup all-purpose flour
2 teaspoons baking powder
¾ teaspoon salt
1 cup milk
1 small onion, minced
1 egg, lightly beaten
   Vegetable oil
   Ketchup (optional)

1. Combine cornmeal, flour, baking powder and salt in medium bowl; mix well. Add milk, onion and egg; stir until well blended. Let batter stand 5 to 10 minutes.

2. Heat 1 inch of oil in large heavy skillet over medium heat to 375°F; adjust heat to maintain temperature. Drop batter by tablespoonfuls into hot oil. Cook, in batches, 2 minutes or until golden brown. Drain on paper towel-lined plate. Serve hush puppies warm with ketchup, if desired.

BROCCOLI AND CHEESE

MAKES 4 TO 6 SERVINGS

2 medium crowns broccoli (1½ pounds), cut into florets (about 6½ cups)

2 tablespoons butter

2 tablespoons all-purpose flour

1½ cups milk

½ teaspoon salt

⅛ teaspoon ground nutmeg

⅛ teaspoon ground red pepper

1 cup (4 ounces) shredded Cheddar cheese

½ cup (2 ounces) shredded Monterey Jack cheese

¼ cup shredded Parmesan cheese

Paprika (optional)

1. Bring large saucepan of water to a boil over medium-high heat. Add broccoli; cook 7 minutes or until tender.

2. Meanwhile, melt butter in medium saucepan over medium-high heat. Add flour; whisk until smooth. Slowly whisk in milk until well blended. Cook 2 minutes or until thickened, whisking frequently. Stir in salt, nutmeg and red pepper. Reduce heat to low; whisk in cheeses in three additions, whisking well after first two additions and stirring just until blended after last addition.

3. Drain broccoli; place on serving plates. Top with cheese sauce; garnish with paprika. Serve immediately.

GARLIC KNOTS

MAKES 20 KNOTS

- 1 package (¼ ounce) active dry yeast
- 1 teaspoon sugar
- ¾ cup warm water (105° to 115°F)
- 2¼ cups all-purpose flour
- 2 tablespoons olive oil, divided
- 1½ teaspoons salt, divided
- 4 tablespoons (½ stick) butter, divided
- 1 tablespoon minced garlic
- ¼ teaspoon garlic powder
- ½ cup grated Parmesan cheese
- 2 tablespoons chopped fresh parsley
- ½ teaspoon dried oregano

1. Dissolve yeast and sugar in warm water in large bowl of stand mixer; let stand 5 minutes or until bubbly. Add flour, 1 tablespoon oil and 1 teaspoon salt; knead with dough hook at low speed 5 minutes or until dough is smooth and elastic.

2. Shape dough into a ball. Place in large greased bowl; turn to grease top. Cover and let rise in warm place 1 hour or until doubled in size.

3. Melt 2 tablespoons butter in small saucepan over low heat. Add remaining 1 tablespoon oil, ½ teaspoon salt, minced garlic and garlic powder; cook over very low heat 5 minutes. Pour into small bowl; set aside.

4. Preheat oven to 400°F. Line baking sheet with parchment paper.

5. Punch down dough. Turn out dough onto lightly floured surface; let rest 10 minutes. Roll out dough into 10×8-inch rectangle; cut into 20 (2-inch) squares. Roll each piece into 8-inch rope; tie in a knot. Place knots on prepared baking sheet; brush with butter mixture.

6. Bake 10 minutes or until lightly browned. Meanwhile, melt remaining 2 tablespoons butter. Combine cheese, parsley and oregano in small bowl; mix well. Brush melted butter over knots immediately after baking; sprinkle with cheese mixture. Cool slightly; serve warm.

**INSPIRED BY
RUTH'S CHRIS®
STEAKHOUSE**

BRUSSELS SPROUTS WITH HONEY BUTTER

MAKES 4 SERVINGS

6 slices thick-cut bacon,
   cut into ½-inch pieces

1½ pounds brussels sprouts
   (about 24 medium),
   halved

¼ teaspoon salt

¼ teaspoon black pepper

2 tablespoons butter,
   softened

2 tablespoons honey

1. Preheat oven to 375°F. Cook bacon in medium skillet until almost crisp. Drain on paper towel-lined plate; set aside. Reserve 1 tablespoon drippings for cooking brussels sprouts.

2. Place brussels sprouts on large baking sheet. Drizzle with reserved bacon drippings and sprinkle with ¼ teaspoon salt and ¼ teaspoon pepper; toss to coat. Spread in single layer on baking sheet.

3. Roast 30 minutes or until brussels sprouts are browned, stirring once.

4. Combine butter and honey in medium bowl; mix well. Add roasted brussels sprouts; stir until completely coated. Stir in bacon; season with additional salt and pepper.

CHICKEN FRIED RICE

MAKES 4 SERVINGS

- 2 tablespoons vegetable oil, divided
- 12 ounces boneless skinless chicken breasts, cut into ½-inch cubes
   Salt and black pepper
- 2 tablespoons butter
- 2 cloves garlic, minced
- ½ sweet onion, diced
- 1 medium carrot, diced
- 2 green onions, thinly sliced
- 3 eggs
- 4 cups cooked rice*
- 3 tablespoons soy sauce
- 2 tablespoons sesame seeds

*For rice, cook 1½ cups rice according to package directions without oil or butter. Spread hot rice on large rimmed baking sheet; cool to room temperature. Refrigerate several hours or overnight. Measure 4 cups for recipe.

1. Heat 1 tablespoon oil in large skillet over medium-high heat. Add chicken; season with salt and pepper. Cook and stir 5 to 6 minutes or until cooked through. Add butter and garlic; cook and stir 1 minute or until butter is melted. Remove to medium bowl.

2. Add sweet onion, carrot and green onions to skillet; cook and stir over high heat 3 minutes or until vegetables are softened. Add to bowl with chicken.

3. Heat remaining 1 tablespoon oil in same skillet. Crack eggs into skillet; cook and stir 45 seconds or until eggs are scrambled but still moist.

4. Add chicken and vegetable mixture, rice, soy sauce and sesame seeds to skillet; cook and stir 2 minutes or until well blended and heated through. Season with additional salt and pepper.

side dishes

CINNAMON APPLES

MAKES 4 SERVINGS

¼ cup (½ stick) butter

3 tart red apples such as Gala, Fuji or Honeycrisp (about 1½ pounds total), peeled and cut into ½-inch wedges

¼ cup packed brown sugar

1 teaspoon ground cinnamon

⅛ teaspoon ground nutmeg

⅛ teaspoon salt

1 tablespoon cornstarch

1. Melt butter in large skillet over medium-high heat. Add apples; cook 8 minutes or until tender, stirring occasionally.

2. Add brown sugar, cinnamon, nutmeg and salt; cook and stir 1 minute or until apples are glazed. Reduce heat to medium-low; stir in cornstarch until well blended.

3. Remove from heat; let stand 5 minutes for glaze to thicken. Stir again; serve immediately.

CHEESY GARLIC BREAD

MAKES 8 TO 10 SERVINGS

side dishes

1 loaf (about 16 ounces) Italian bread

½ cup (1 stick) butter, softened

8 cloves garlic, very thinly sliced

¼ cup grated Parmesan cheese

2 cups (8 ounces) shredded mozzarella cheese

1. Preheat oven to 425°F. Line large baking sheet with foil.

2. Cut bread in half horizontally. Spread cut sides of bread evenly with butter; top with sliced garlic. Sprinkle with Parmesan, then mozzarella. Place on prepared baking sheet.

3. Bake 12 minutes or until cheeses are melted and golden brown in spots. Cut bread crosswise into slices. Serve warm.

CAJUN RICE

MAKES 8 TO 10 SERVINGS

- 2 cups uncooked long grain rice
- 4 cups water, divided
- 1¼ teaspoons salt, divided
- 4 green onions, finely chopped, green and white parts separated
- 8 ounces ground beef
- 8 ounces chicken gizzards, minced*
- ½ cup finely chopped green bell pepper
- 1 teaspoon Cajun or Creole seasoning
- ½ teaspoon garlic powder
- ¼ teaspoon celery seed
- ¼ teaspoon ground red pepper
- ¼ teaspoon black pepper

Or substitute an additional 8 ounces ground beef for the chicken gizzards.

1. Rinse rice in strainer under cool running water; drain. Combine rice, 3¾ cups water and 1 teaspoon salt in medium saucepan; bring to a boil over medium-high heat. Reduce heat to low; cover and cook about 17 minutes or until liquid is absorbed and rice is tender but still firm. Remove from heat; let stand, covered, 5 minutes. Fluff rice with fork; stir in green parts of green onions.

2. Meanwhile, cook beef in large deep skillet over medium-high heat 5 minutes until beef is cooked through, stirring frequently. Remove to plate; drain fat.

3. Add chicken gizzards and bell pepper to skillet; cook 7 minutes or until chicken is cooked through. Add white parts of green onions, Cajun seasoning, garlic powder, celery seed, red pepper, black pepper and remaining ¼ teaspoon salt; cook and stir 2 minutes. Return beef to skillet; mix well.

4. Stir in rice and remaining ¼ cup water; cook over medium-low heat 15 minutes, stirring occasionally.

HEARTY HASH BROWN CASSEROLE

MAKES ABOUT 16 SERVINGS

- 2 cups sour cream
- 2 cups (8 ounces) shredded Colby cheese, divided
- 1 can (10¾ ounces) cream of chicken soup
- ½ cup (1 stick) butter, melted
- 1 small onion, finely chopped
- ¾ teaspoon salt
- ½ teaspoon black pepper
- 1 package (30 ounces) frozen shredded hash brown potatoes, thawed

1. Preheat oven to 375°F. Spray 13×9-inch baking dish with nonstick cooking spray.

2. Combine sour cream, 1½ cups cheese, soup, butter, onion, salt and pepper in large bowl; mix well. Add potatoes; stir until well blended. Spread mixture in prepared baking dish. (Do not pack down.) Sprinkle with remaining ½ cup cheese.

3. Bake 45 minutes or until cheese is melted and top of casserole is beginning to brown.

desserts

CHOCOLATE STORM

MAKES 9 SERVINGS

INSPIRED BY OUTBACK STEAKHOUSE®

- 12 ounces semisweet chocolate, chopped
- 12 ounces bittersweet chocolate, chopped
- ¾ cup (1½ sticks) butter
- 5 eggs
- ⅔ cup granulated sugar
- 2 teaspoons vanilla
- ½ teaspoon salt
- 1¼ cups chopped pecans
- 2 cups cold whipping cream
- ¼ cup powdered sugar
- 3 pints vanilla ice cream
- 1½ cups hot fudge topping, heated
- Chocolate curls (optional)

1. Preheat oven to 325°F. Spray 9-inch square baking pan with nonstick cooking spray.

2. Combine semisweet chocolate, bittersweet chocolate and butter in medium microwavable bowl. Microwave on HIGH 1 minute; stir and repeat. Microwave 30 seconds; stir until chocolate is melted and mixture is smooth.

3. Beat eggs, granulated sugar, vanilla and salt in large bowl with electric mixer at medium speed 1 minute. Beat at high speed 1 minute. Add half of chocolate mixture; beat at low speed until blended. Beat in remaining chocolate mixture until blended. Stir in pecans. Pour batter into prepared pan, spreading to make top of cake level and smooth.

4. Bake about 45 minutes or until center begins to firm. Cool in pan on wire rack.

5. When ready to serve, beat cream and powdered sugar in medium bowl with electric mixer at medium-high speed until stiff peaks form. Cut cake into 9 squares. If desired, heat individual squares in microwave on HIGH 30 seconds. Top with ice cream, hot fudge, whipped cream and chocolate curls, if desired.

WARM APPLE CROSTATA

MAKES 4 TARTS (4 TO 8 SERVINGS)

- 1¾ cups all-purpose flour
- ⅓ cup granulated sugar
- ½ teaspoon plus ⅛ teaspoon salt, divided
- ¾ cup (1½ sticks) cold butter, cut into small pieces
- 3 tablespoons ice water
- 2 teaspoons vanilla
- 8 Pink Lady or Honeycrisp apples (about 1½ pounds), peeled and cut into ¼-inch slices
- ¼ cup packed brown sugar
- 1 tablespoon lemon juice
- 1 teaspoon ground cinnamon
- ⅛ teaspoon ground nutmeg
- 4 teaspoons butter, cut into very small pieces
- 1 egg, beaten
- 1 to 2 teaspoons coarse sugar
  Vanilla ice cream
  Caramel sauce or ice cream topping

1. Combine flour, granulated sugar and ½ teaspoon salt in food processor; process 5 seconds. Add ¾ cup cold butter; process about 10 seconds or until mixture resembles coarse crumbs.

2. Combine ice water and vanilla in small bowl. With motor running, pour mixture through feed tube; process 12 seconds or until dough begins to come together. Shape dough into a disc; wrap with plastic wrap and refrigerate 30 minutes.

3. Meanwhile, combine apples, brown sugar, lemon juice, cinnamon, nutmeg and remaining ⅛ teaspoon salt in large bowl; toss to coat. Preheat oven to 400°F.

4. Line two baking sheets with parchment paper. Cut dough into four pieces; roll out each piece into 7-inch circle on floured surface. Place on prepared baking sheets; mound apples in center of dough circles (about 1 cup apples for each crostata). Fold or roll up edges of dough towards center to create rim of crostata. Dot apples with 4 teaspoons butter. Brush dough with egg; sprinkle dough and apples with coarse sugar.

5. Bake about 20 minutes or until apples are tender and crust is golden brown. Serve warm topped with ice cream and caramel sauce.

KEY LIME PIE

MAKES 8 SERVINGS

12 whole graham crackers*

⅓ cup butter, melted

3 tablespoons sugar

2 cans (14 ounces each)
   sweetened condensed
   milk

¾ cup key lime juice

6 egg yolks

   Pinch salt

   Whipped cream (optional)

   Lime slices (optional)

*Or substitute 1½ cups
graham cracker crumbs.*

1. Preheat oven to 350°F. Spray 9-inch pie plate or springform pan with nonstick cooking spray.

2. Place graham crackers in food processor; pulse until coarse crumbs form. Add butter and sugar; pulse until well blended. Press mixture onto bottom and 1 inch up side of prepared pie plate. Bake 8 minutes or until lightly browned. Remove to wire rack to cool 10 minutes. *Reduce oven temperature to 325°F.*

3. Meanwhile, beat sweetened condensed milk, lime juice, egg yolks and salt in large bowl with electric mixer at medium-low speed 1 minute or until well blended and smooth. Pour into crust.

4. Bake 20 minutes or until top is set. Cool completely on wire rack. Cover and refrigerate 2 hours or overnight. Garnish with whipped cream and lime slices.

INSPIRED BY TGI FRIDAYSᴿᴹ

TOFFEE CAKE WITH WHISKEY SAUCE

MAKES 9 SERVINGS

8 ounces chopped dates

2¼ teaspoons baking soda, divided

1½ cups boiling water

2 cups all-purpose flour

½ teaspoon salt

¾ cup (1½ sticks) butter, softened

½ cup granulated sugar

½ cup packed dark brown sugar

2 eggs

1 teaspoon vanilla

1½ cups butterscotch sauce

2 tablespoons whiskey

1 cup glazed pecans* or chopped toasted pecans

Vanilla ice cream

Glazed or candied pecans may be found in the produce section of the supermarket with other salad toppings, or they may be found in the snack aisle.

1. Preheat oven to 350°F. Spray 9-inch square baking pan with nonstick cooking spray.

2. Combine dates and 1½ teaspoons baking soda in medium bowl. Stir in boiling water; let stand 10 minutes to soften. Mash with fork or process in food processor until mixture forms paste.

3. Combine flour, remaining ¾ teaspoon baking soda and salt in medium bowl; mix well. Beat butter, granulated sugar and brown sugar in large bowl with electric mixer at medium speed 3 minutes or until creamy. Add eggs, one at a time, beating until well blended after each addition. Beat in vanilla. Add flour mixture alternately with date mixture at low speed; beat just until blended. Spread batter in prepared pan.

4. Bake about 30 minutes or until toothpick inserted into center comes out with moist crumbs. Cool in pan on wire rack 15 minutes.

5. Place butterscotch sauce in medium microwavable bowl; microwave on HIGH 30 seconds or until warm. Stir in whiskey. Drizzle sauce over each serving; sprinkle with pecans and top with ice cream.

STRAWBERRY CHEESECAKE DESSERT SHOOTERS

MAKES 8 TO 10 SERVINGS

desserts

- 1 cup graham cracker crumbs, plus additional for garnish
- ¼ cup (½ stick) butter, melted
- 2 cups chopped fresh strawberries
- ¾ cup sugar, divided
- 12 ounces cream cheese, softened
- 2 eggs
- 2 tablespoons sour cream
- ½ teaspoon vanilla
- Whipped cream

1. Place 1 cup graham cracker crumbs in medium nonstick skillet; cook and stir over medium heat about 3 minutes or until lightly browned. Transfer to small bowl; stir in butter until well blended. Press mixture evenly into 8 to 10 (3- to 4-ounce) shot glasses.

2. Combine strawberries and ¼ cup sugar in small bowl; toss to coat. Cover and refrigerate until ready to serve.

3. Beat cream cheese in medium bowl with electric mixer at medium speed until creamy. Add eggs, remaining ½ cup sugar, sour cream and vanilla; beat until well blended. Transfer to medium saucepan; cook over medium heat 5 to 6 minutes or until thickened and smooth, stirring frequently. Divide mixture evenly among prepared crusts. Refrigerate 1 hour or until cold.

4. Top each serving with strawberries and whipped cream. Garnish with additional graham cracker crumbs.

/////////////////////////////////

tip

For larger servings, use four to five 6- or 8-ounce juice or stemless wine glasses. Divide crumb mixture, filling and strawberries evenly among glasses.

MARBLED COOKIE BROWNIE

MAKES 9 TO 12 SERVINGS

desserts

- 1 cup plus 1 tablespoon all-purpose flour
- ½ teaspoon baking soda
- ½ teaspoon salt
- ½ cup (1 stick) butter, softened
- ½ cup packed brown sugar
- ¼ cup granulated sugar
- 1 egg
- ½ teaspoon vanilla
- 1 cup milk chocolate chunks or chips
- 1 package (18 to 19 ounces) brownie mix, plus ingredients to prepare mix

1. Preheat oven to 350°F. Line 9-inch square baking pan with parchment paper; spray paper with nonstick cooking spray.

2. For cookies, combine flour, baking soda and salt in small bowl; mix well. Beat butter, brown sugar and granulated sugar in large bowl with electric mixer at medium speed about 3 minutes or until light and fluffy, scraping down side of bowl occasionally. Add egg; beat until well blended. Beat in vanilla. Gradually add flour mixture; beat at low speed just until blended. Stir in chocolate chunks. Cover and refrigerate dough while preparing brownies.

3. Prepare brownie mix according to package directions. Spread batter in prepared pan; smooth top. Scoop out eight 1½-tablespoon balls of cookie dough; roll into smooth, round balls. (Reserve remaining cookie dough for another use.) Scatter cookie dough balls over brownie batter; press down gently to push cookie dough into brownie batter.

4. Bake 25 minutes, then cover loosely with foil to prevent cookies from becoming too brown. Bake about 13 minutes or until brownies are firm, edges begin to come away from side of pan and toothpick inserted into center comes out clean. Cool in pan on wire rack 10 minutes. Serve warm or at room temperature.

TIRAMISU

MAKES 9 SERVINGS

¾   cup sugar

4   egg yolks

1   cup plus 2 tablespoons
    whipping cream, divided

16   ounces mascarpone
    cheese

½   teaspoon vanilla

¾   cup cold strong brewed
    coffee

¼   cup coffee-flavored liqueur

24   to 28 ladyfingers

2   teaspoons unsweetened
    cocoa powder

1. Fill medium saucepan half full with water; bring to a boil over high heat. Reduce heat to low to maintain a simmer. Whisk sugar, egg yolks and 2 tablespoons cream in medium metal bowl until well blended. Place bowl over simmering water; cook 6 to 8 minutes or until thickened, whisking constantly. Remove from heat; cool slightly. Whisk in mascarpone and vanilla until smooth and well blended.

2. Pour remaining 1 cup cream into large bowl of stand mixer; beat at high speed until stiff peaks form. Gently fold whipped cream into mascarpone mixture until no streaks of white remain.

3. Combine coffee and liqueur in shallow bowl; mix well. Working with one ladyfinger at a time, dip cookies briefly into coffee mixture. Arrange in single layer in 9-inch square baking pan, trimming cookies to fit as necessary.

4. Spread thin layer of custard over ladyfingers, covering completely. Dip remaining ladyfingers in remaining coffee mixture; arrange in single layer over custard. Spread remaining custard over cookies. Place cocoa in fine-mesh strainer; sprinkle over custard. Refrigerate 2 hours or overnight.

CLASSIC FLAN

MAKES 6 SERVINGS

INSPIRED BY
CHEVYS
FRESH MEX®

desserts

1½ cups sugar, divided

1 tablespoon water

¼ teaspoon ground
cinnamon

3 cups whole milk

3 eggs

3 egg yolks

1 teaspoon vanilla

1. Preheat oven to 300°F.

2. Combine 1 cup sugar, water and cinnamon in medium saucepan; cook over medium-high heat without stirring about 10 minutes or until sugar is melted and mixture is deep golden amber in color. Pour into six 6-ounce ramekins, swirling to coat bottoms. Place ramekins in 13×9-inch baking pan.

3. Heat milk in separate medium saucepan over medium heat until bubbles begin to form around edge of pan.

4. Meanwhile, whisk eggs, egg yolks, vanilla and remaining ½ cup sugar in medium bowl until well blended. Whisk in ½ cup hot milk in thin, steady stream. Gradually whisk in remaining milk. Divide milk mixture evenly among ramekins. Carefully add hot water to baking pan until water comes halfway up sides of ramekins. Cover ramekins with waxed paper or parchment paper.

5. Bake 1 hour 15 minutes or until custard is firm and knife inserted into custard comes out clean. Remove ramekins from baking pan to wire rack; cool completely. Cover and refrigerate until cold. Run small knife around edges of ramekins; invert flan onto serving plates.

RASPBERRY WHITE CHOCOLATE CHEESECAKE

MAKES 12 SERVINGS

24 chocolate sandwich cookies, crushed into fine crumbs

3 tablespoons butter, melted

4 packages (8 ounces each) cream cheese, softened

1¼ cups sugar

½ cup sour cream

2 teaspoons vanilla

5 eggs, at room temperature

1 bar (4 ounces) white chocolate, chopped into ¼-inch pieces

¾ cup seedless raspberry jam, stirred

Shaved white chocolate

Whipped cream and fresh raspberries

1. Preheat oven to 350°F. Spray 9-inch springform pan with nonstick cooking spray. Line bottom and side of pan with parchment paper. Wrap outside of pan tightly with foil.

2. For crust, combine crushed cookies and butter in small bowl; mix well. Press mixture onto bottom and 1 inch up side of prepared pan. Bake about 8 minutes or until firm. Remove to wire rack to cool completely. *Increase oven temperature to 450°F.*

3. Beat cream cheese in large bowl with electric mixer at low speed until creamy. Add sugar, sour cream and vanilla; beat until smooth and well blended. Add eggs, one at a time, beating until well blended after each addition. Fold in chopped white chocolate with spatula. Spread one third of filling in crust. Drop half of jam by teaspoonfuls over filling; swirl gently with small knife or skewer, being careful not to overmix. Top with one third of filling; drop remaining jam by teaspoonfuls over filling and gently swirl jam. Spread remaining filling over top.

4. Place springform pan in large roasting pan; fill roasting pan with hot water to come about halfway up side of springform pan. Carefully place in oven. *Immediately reduce oven temperature to 350°F.* Bake about 1 hour 10 minutes or until top of cheesecake is lightly browned and center jiggles slightly.

5. Remove cheesecake from roasting pan to wire rack; remove foil. Cool to room temperature. Cover and refrigerate 4 hours or overnight. Top with shaved white chocolate, whipped cream and raspberries.

desserts

FRENCH SILK PIE

MAKES 8 SERVINGS

desserts

- 1 9-inch deep-dish pie crust (frozen or refrigerated)
- 1⅓ cups granulated sugar
- ¾ cup (1½ sticks) butter, softened
- 4 ounces unsweetened chocolate, melted
- 1½ tablespoons unsweetened cocoa powder
- 1 teaspoon vanilla
- ⅛ teaspoon salt
- 4 pasteurized eggs*
- 1 cup whipping cream
- 2 tablespoons powdered sugar

Chocolate curls (optional)

*The eggs in this recipe are not cooked, so use pasteurized eggs to ensure food safety.

1. Bake pie crust according to package directions. Cool completely on wire rack.

2. Beat granulated sugar and butter in large bowl with electric mixer at medium speed about 4 minutes or until light and fluffy. Add melted chocolate, cocoa, vanilla and salt; beat until well blended. Add eggs, one at a time, beating 4 minutes after each addition and scraping down side of bowl occasionally.

3. Spread filling in cooled crust; refrigerate at least 3 hours or overnight.

4. Beat cream and powdered sugar in medium bowl with electric mixer at high speed until soft peaks form. Pipe or spread whipped cream over chocolate layer; garnish with chocolate curls.

INSPIRED BY STARBUCKS®

GLAZED LEMON LOAF

MAKES 8 TO 10 SERVINGS

CAKE

1½ cups all-purpose flour
½ teaspoon baking powder
½ teaspoon baking soda
½ teaspoon salt
1 cup granulated sugar
3 eggs
½ cup vegetable oil
⅓ cup lemon juice
2 tablespoons butter, melted
1 teaspoon lemon extract
½ teaspoon vanilla

GLAZE

3 tablespoons butter
1½ cups powdered sugar
2 tablespoons lemon juice
1 to 2 teaspoons grated lemon peel

1. Preheat oven to 350°F. Grease and flour 8×4-inch loaf pan.

2. For cake, combine flour, baking powder, baking soda and salt in large bowl; mix well. Whisk granulated sugar, eggs, oil, ⅓ cup lemon juice, 2 tablespoons melted butter, lemon extract and vanilla in medium bowl until well blended. Add to flour mixture; stir just until blended. Pour batter into prepared pan.

3. Bake about 40 minutes or until toothpick inserted into center comes out clean. Cool in pan 10 minutes; remove to wire rack to cool 10 minutes.

4. Meanwhile, prepare glaze. Melt 3 tablespoons butter in small saucepan over medium-low heat. Whisk in powdered sugar, 2 tablespoons lemon juice and 1 teaspoon lemon peel; cook until smooth and hot, whisking constantly. Pour glaze over warm cake; smooth top. Cool completely before slicing. Garnish with additional 1 teaspoon lemon peel, if desired.

ICE CREAM PIZZA TREAT

MAKES 8 SERVINGS

24 chocolate sandwich
     cookies

1 jar (about 12 ounces)
    hot fudge ice cream
    topping, divided

2 pints vanilla ice cream

⅓ cup candy-coated
    chocolate pieces

1. Place cookies in food processor; pulse until large crumbs form. (Do not overprocess into fine crumbs.) Add ½ cup hot fudge topping; pulse just until blended. (Mixture should not be smooth; small cookie pieces may remain.)

2. Transfer mixture to pizza pan; press into 11- to 12-circle about ¼ inch thick. Freeze crust 10 minutes. Meanwhile, remove ice cream from freezer to soften 10 minutes.

3. Spread ice cream evenly over crust (about ½-inch-thick layer), leaving ½-inch border. Return to freezer; freeze 2 hours or until firm.

4. Heat remaining hot fudge topping according to package directions. Drizzle over ice cream; top with chocolate pieces. Freeze 1 hour or until firm. Cut into wedges to serve.

desserts

RED VELVET CAKE

MAKES 8 TO 10 SERVINGS

desserts

280

CAKE

- 2 cups all-purpose flour
- 2 tablespoons unsweetened cocoa powder
- 1 teaspoon salt
- 1¼ cups buttermilk
- 1 bottle (1 ounce) red food coloring
- 1 teaspoon vanilla
- 1½ cups granulated sugar
- 1 cup (2 sticks) butter, softened
- 2 eggs
- 1 tablespoon white or cider vinegar
- 1½ teaspoons baking soda

FROSTING

- 2 packages (8 ounces each) cream cheese, softened
- ½ cup (1 stick) butter, softened
- 6 cups powdered sugar
- ¼ cup milk
- 2 teaspoons vanilla
- 4 ounces white chocolate, shaved with vegetable peeler

1. Preheat oven to 350°F. Spray three 9-inch cake pans with nonstick cooking spray. Line bottoms of pans with parchment paper; spray paper with cooking spray.

2. For cake, combine flour, cocoa and salt in medium bowl. Combine buttermilk, food coloring and vanilla in small bowl; mix well.

3. Beat granulated sugar and 1 cup butter in large bowl with electric mixer at medium speed 5 minutes or until light and fluffy. Add eggs, one at a time, beating until well blended after each addition. Add flour mixture alternately with buttermilk mixture, beating at low speed after each addition. Stir vinegar into baking soda in small bowl. Add to batter; stir gently until blended. Pour batter into prepared pans.

4. Bake about 20 minutes or until toothpick inserted into centers comes out clean. Cool in pans 10 minutes. Invert onto wire racks; peel off parchment. Cool completely.

5. For frosting, beat cream cheese and ½ cup butter in large bowl with electric mixer at medium speed until creamy. Add powdered sugar, milk and 2 teaspoons vanilla; beat at low speed until blended. Beat at medium speed until smooth.

6. Place one cake layer on serving plate; spread with 1½ cups frosting. Top with second cake layer; spread with 1½ cups frosting. Top with remaining cake layer; spread remaining frosting over top and side of cake. Press white chocolate shavings onto side of cake.

DOUBLE CHOCOLATE COOKIES AND CREAM MOUSSE

MAKES 8 SERVINGS

desserts

- 8 ounces semisweet chocolate, chopped
- 2½ cups chilled whipping cream, divided
- 4 egg yolks
  Pinch salt
- 1¼ teaspoons vanilla, divided
- ¼ cup granulated sugar
- 23 chocolate sandwich cookies, divided
- 1 tablespoon powdered sugar

1. Melt chocolate in medium saucepan over very low heat, stirring frequently. Remove from heat; stir in ¼ cup cream until well blended.

2. Combine egg yolks and pinch of salt in medium bowl. Whisk about half of chocolate mixture into egg yolks until blended; whisk egg yolk mixture back into chocolate mixture in saucepan. Cook over low heat 2 minutes, whisking constantly. Remove from heat; cool to room temperature.

3. Beat 1¾ cups cream and 1 teaspoon vanilla in large bowl with electric mixer at high speed until soft peaks form. Slowly beat in granulated sugar; continue beating until stiff peaks form. Fold about one fourth of whipped cream into chocolate mixture; fold chocolate mixture into remaining whipped cream until completely combined.

4. Finely chop 2 cookies; fold into mousse. Coarsely chop 2 cookies for topping. Cut remaining 19 cookies into quarters; set aside. Refrigerate mousse 4 hours or overnight.

5. Beat remaining ½ cup cream in medium bowl with electric mixer at high speed 30 seconds or until thickened. Add powdered sugar and remaining ¼ teaspoon vanilla; beat until stiff peaks form.

6. Spoon ¼ cup mousse into each of eight wide-mouth half-pint jars. Top with ¼ cup quartered cookies and another ¼ cup mousse. Garnish with dollop of sweetened whipped cream and chopped cookies.

BANANA CREAM PIE

MAKES 8 SERVINGS

- 1 refrigerated pie crust (half of a 15-ounce package), at room temperature
- ⅔ cup sugar
- ¼ cup cornstarch
- ¼ teaspoon salt
- 2½ cups milk
- 4 egg yolks, beaten
- 2 tablespoons butter, softened
- 2 teaspoons vanilla
- 2 medium bananas
- 1 teaspoon lemon juice

  Whipped cream and toasted sliced almonds (optional)

1. Preheat oven to 400°F. Line 9-inch pie plate with crust; flute edge. Prick bottom and side all over with fork. Bake 10 minutes or until crust is golden brown. Cool completely on wire rack.

2. Combine sugar, cornstarch and salt in medium saucepan. Whisk in milk until well blended. Cook over medium heat about 12 minutes or until mixture boils and thickens, stirring constantly. Boil 2 minutes, stirring constantly. Remove from heat.

3. Slowly whisk ½ hot cup milk mixture into egg yolks in small bowl. Slowly whisk mixture back into milk mixture in saucepan. Cook over medium heat about 5 minutes, whisking constantly. Remove from heat; whisk in butter and vanilla. Cool 20 minutes, stirring occasionally. Strain through fine-mesh strainer into medium bowl. Press plastic wrap onto surface of pudding; cool about 30 minutes or until lukewarm.

4. Cut bananas into ¼-inch slices; toss with lemon juice in medium bowl. Spread half of pudding in cooled crust; arrange bananas over pudding. (Reserve several slices for garnish, if desired.) Spread remaining pudding over bananas. Refrigerate 4 hours or overnight. Garnish with whipped cream, almonds and reserved banana slices.

CARROT CAKE

MAKES 8 TO 10 SERVINGS

desserts

CAKE

- 2 cups all-purpose flour
- 2 teaspoons baking soda
- 2 teaspoons ground cinnamon
- 1 teaspoon salt
- 4 eggs
- 2¼ cups granulated sugar
- 1 cup vegetable oil
- 1 cup buttermilk
- 1 tablespoon vanilla
- 3 medium carrots, shredded (3 cups)
- 3 cups walnuts, chopped and toasted,* divided
- 1 cup shredded coconut
- 1 can (8 ounces) crushed pineapple

FROSTING

- 2 packages (8 ounces each) cream cheese, softened
- 1 cup (2 sticks) butter, softened
- Pinch salt
- 3 cups powdered sugar
- 1 tablespoon orange juice
- 2 teaspoons grated orange peel
- 1 teaspoon vanilla

*To toast walnuts, spread on ungreased baking sheet. Bake in preheated 350°F oven 6 to 8 minutes or until lightly browned, stirring frequently.

1. Preheat oven to 350°F. Spray two 9-inch round cake pans with nonstick cooking spray. Line bottoms of pans with parchment paper; spray paper with cooking spray.

2. For cake, combine flour, baking soda, cinnamon and 1 teaspoon salt in medium bowl; mix well. Whisk eggs in large bowl until blended. Add granulated sugar, oil, buttermilk and 1 tablespoon vanilla; whisk until well blended. Add flour mixture; stir until well blended. Add carrots, 1 cup walnuts, coconut and pineapple; stir just until blended. Pour batter into prepared pans.

3. Bake 25 to 30 minutes or until toothpick inserted into centers comes out clean. Cool in pans 10 minutes; remove to wire racks to cool completely.

4. For frosting, beat cream cheese, butter and pinch of salt in large bowl with electric mixer at medium speed 3 minutes or until creamy. Add powdered sugar, orange juice, orange peel and 1 teaspoon vanilla; beat at low speed until blended. Beat at medium speed 2 minutes or until frosting is smooth.

5. Place one cake layer on serving plate; spread with 2 cups frosting. Top with second cake layer; frost top and side of cake with remaining frosting. Press 1¾ cups walnuts onto side of cake. Sprinkle remaining ¼ cup walnuts over top of cake.

BROWNIE LASAGNA

MAKES 6 TO 12 SERVINGS

BROWNIE

- ¾ cup unsweetened cocoa powder
- ¾ cup (1½ sticks) butter, melted
- 1⅓ cups all-purpose flour
- ½ teaspoon baking powder
- ½ teaspoon salt
- ½ teaspoon espresso powder or instant coffee granules
- 1⅔ cups granulated sugar
- 2 tablespoons vegetable oil
- 2 tablespoons water
- 3 eggs
- 1 teaspoon vanilla

FROSTING

- 1 package (8 ounces) cream cheese, softened
- ½ cup (1 stick) butter, softened
- 2½ cups powdered sugar
- 2 teaspoons vanilla
- Chocolate shavings (optional)
- Hot fudge topping or chocolate sauce, warmed

1. For brownie, preheat oven to 350°F. Line 13×9-inch baking pan with parchment paper or spray generously with nonstick cooking spray.

2. Stir cocoa into warm melted butter in large bowl until well blended and smooth; let stand 5 minutes. Combine flour, baking powder, salt and espresso powder in medium bowl; mix well. Add granulated sugar, oil and water to cocoa mixture; stir until well blended. Beat in eggs, one at a time, until blended. Stir in 1 teaspoon vanilla. Add flour mixture; stir until blended. Spread batter evenly in prepared pan.

3. Bake about 18 minutes or until toothpick inserted into center comes out with fudgy crumbs. Cool completely in pan on wire rack. Cover and refrigerate 4 hours or overnight. (Chilled brownies are easier to cut.)

4. For frosting, beat cream cheese and softened butter in large bowl with electric mixer at medium speed about 3 minutes or until creamy. Add powdered sugar and 2 teaspoons vanilla; beat at low speed until blended. Beat at medium speed 2 minutes or until smooth.

5. Remove brownie from pan; place on cutting board. Cut in half crosswise, then cut each piece in half horizontally with serrated knife to create total of four thin layers.

6. Place one brownie layer on serving plate; spread with ⅔ cup frosting. Repeat layers three times. Refrigerate at least 2 hours before serving. Top with chocolate shavings, if desired; drizzle with hot fudge topping.

PUMPKIN CHEESECAKE

MAKES 12 SERVINGS

CRUST

- 18 graham crackers (2 sleeves)
- ¼ cup sugar
- ⅛ teaspoon salt
- ½ cup (1 stick) butter, melted

FILLING

- 1 can (15 ounces) pure pumpkin
- ¼ cup sour cream
- 2 teaspoons vanilla
- 2 teaspoons ground cinnamon, plus additional for garnish
- 1 teaspoon ground ginger
- ¼ teaspoon salt
- ¼ teaspoon ground cloves
- 4 packages (8 ounces each) cream cheese, softened
- 1¾ cups sugar
- 5 eggs
- Whipped cream

1. Line bottom of 9-inch springform pan with parchment paper. Spray bottom and side of pan with nonstick cooking spray. Wrap outside of pan with heavy-duty foil.

2. For crust, place graham crackers in food processor; pulse until fine crumbs form. Add ¼ cup sugar and ⅛ teaspoon salt; pulse to blend. Add butter; pulse until crumbs are moistened and mixture is well blended. Press onto bottom and all the way up side of prepared pan in thin layer. Refrigerate at least 20 minutes. Preheat oven to 350°F.

3. Bake crust 12 minutes; cool on wire rack. Bring large pot of water to a boil.

4. For filling, whisk pumpkin, sour cream, vanilla, 2 teaspoons cinnamon, ginger, ¼ teaspoon salt and cloves in medium bowl until well blended. Beat cream cheese and 1¾ cups sugar in large bowl with electric mixer at medium speed until smooth and creamy. With mixer running, beat in eggs, one at a time, until blended. Scrape side of bowl. Add pumpkin mixture; beat at medium speed until well blended. Pour into crust. Place springform pan in large roasting pan; place in oven. Carefully add boiling water to roasting pan to come about halfway up side of springform pan.

5. Bake 1 hour 15 minutes or until top is set and lightly browned and center jiggles slightly. Remove cheesecake from roasting pan to wire rack; remove foil. Cool to room temperature. Run small thin spatula around edge of pan to loosen crust. (Do not remove side of pan.) Cover with plastic wrap; refrigerate 8 hours or overnight. Garnish with whipped cream and additional cinnamon.

desserts

CHOCOLATE ECLAIR CAKE

MAKES 12 TO 18 SERVINGS

3¼ cups plus 6 tablespoons whole milk, divided

2 packages (3.4 ounces each) vanilla instant pudding and pie filling mix

1 container (8 ounces) frozen whipped topping, thawed

1⅓ boxes (about 14 ounces each) graham crackers (35 whole graham cracker rectangles)

6 tablespoons (¾ stick) butter

⅓ cup unsweetened dark or regular cocoa powder

Pinch salt

1 teaspoon vanilla

2 cups powdered sugar, sifted

1. Whisk 3¼ cups milk and vanilla pudding mixes in large bowl about 2 minutes. Fold in whipped topping until well blended.

2. Cover bottom of 13×9-inch pan with single layer of graham crackers, cutting to fit as needed. Pour one third of pudding mixture (about 2½ cups) over graham crackers; smooth top with spatula. Repeat layers twice. Top with remaining graham crackers, arranging them bumpy side down over pudding mixture.

3. Combine remaining 6 tablespoons milk and butter in large microwavable bowl; microwave on HIGH 30 seconds. Stir; microwave 30 seconds or until butter is melted. Add cocoa and salt; whisk until blended. Stir in vanilla. Add powdered sugar; whisk until well blended and smooth.

4. Pour chocolate icing over graham crackers, spreading evenly and covering top completely. Refrigerate 8 hours or overnight.

SWEET POTATO PECAN PIE

MAKES 8 SERVINGS

desserts

- 1 sweet potato (about 1 pound)
- 3 eggs, divided
- 8 tablespoons granulated sugar, divided
- 8 tablespoons packed brown sugar, divided
- 2 tablespoons butter, melted, divided
- ½ teaspoon ground cinnamon
- ½ teaspoon salt, divided
- 1 frozen 9-inch deep-dish pie crust
- ½ cup dark corn syrup
- 1½ teaspoons lemon juice
- 1½ teaspoons vanilla
- 1 cup pecan halves
- Vanilla ice cream (optional)

1. Preheat oven to 350°F. Prick sweet potato all over with fork. Bake 1 hour or until fork-tender; let stand until cool enough to handle. Peel sweet potato and place in bowl of stand mixer. *Reduce oven temperature to 300°F.*

2. Add 1 egg, 2 tablespoons granulated sugar, 2 tablespoons brown sugar, 1 tablespoon butter, cinnamon and ¼ teaspoon salt to bowl with sweet potato; beat at medium speed 5 minutes or until smooth and fluffy. Spread mixture in frozen pie crust; place in refrigerator.

3. Combine remaining 6 tablespoons granulated sugar, 6 tablespoons brown sugar, 1 tablespoon butter, ¼ teaspoon salt, corn syrup, lemon juice and vanilla in clean mixer bowl; beat at medium speed 5 minutes. Add remaining 2 eggs; beat 5 minutes.

4. Place crust on baking sheet. Spread pecans over sweet potato filling; pour corn syrup mixture evenly over pecans.

5. Bake 1 hour or until center is set and top is deep golden brown. Cool completely on wire rack. Serve with ice cream, if desired.

LIMONCELLO CAKE WITH MASCARPONE FROSTING

MAKES 8 TO 10 SERVINGS

desserts

CAKE

- 2½ cups all-purpose flour
- 1 teaspoon baking powder
- 1 teaspoon baking soda
- ¾ teaspoon salt
- 2 cups granulated sugar
- ¾ cup (1½ sticks) butter, softened
- 4 eggs
- 3 tablespoons grated lemon peel
- ¾ cup buttermilk
- ½ cup lemon juice
- ½ cup plus 1 tablespoon limoncello, divided
- Yellow food coloring (optional)

FROSTING

- 1 cup whipping cream
- ¼ cup powdered sugar
- 1 container (8 ounces) mascarpone cheese
- 2 tablespoons granulated sugar
- 3 tablespoons lemon juice
- White chocolate shavings (optional)

1. For cake, preheat oven to 350°F. Line bottoms of two 9-inch round baking pans with parchment paper; grease and flour pans. Combine flour, baking powder, baking soda and salt in medium bowl; mix well.

2. Beat 2 cups granulated sugar and butter in large bowl with electric mixer at medium-high speed 5 minutes or until light and fluffy. Add eggs, one at a time, beating 30 seconds after each addition. Scrape bottom and side of bowl. Add lemon peel; beat at medium-high speed 1 minute.

3. Combine buttermilk and lemon juice in 2-cup measure. With mixer at low speed, alternately add flour mixture, buttermilk mixture and ½ cup limoncello, beginning and ending with flour mixture. Tint batter with food coloring, if desired. Stir with spatula until well blended. Pour batter into prepared pans; smooth top.

4. Bake 25 to 30 minutes or until tops are golden brown and toothpick inserted into centers comes out clean. Cool in pans 10 minutes; remove to wire racks to cool completely.

5. For frosting, beat cream and powdered sugar in large bowl with electric mixer with whip attachment at medium-high speed 2 minutes or until stiff peaks form. Transfer to medium bowl. Combine mascarpone, 2 tablespoons granulated sugar and 3 tablespoons lemon juice in same large bowl. Replace whip with paddle attachment; beat at medium speed 2 minutes or until smooth and well blended. Stir one third of whipped cream into mascarpone mixture. Gently fold in remaining whipped cream until well blended.

6. Place one cake layer on serving plate; brush with half of remaining 1 tablespoon limoncello. Spread half of frosting over cake. Top with second cake layer; brush with remaining limoncello. Spread remaining frosting over top of cake. Garnish with white chocolate shavings.

beverages

INSPIRED BY WENDY'S®

CHOCOLATE FROSTY

MAKES 2 TO 3 SERVINGS

- 2 cups milk, divided
- ¼ cup unsweetened cocoa powder
- ½ cup sweetened condensed milk
- 1 tablespoon corn syrup
- 1 teaspoon vanilla

1. Whisk ¼ cup milk and cocoa in large measuring cup with pour spout until well blended. Whisk in 1½ cups milk, sweetened condensed milk, corn syrup and vanilla. Pour mixture into ice cube tray. Freeze 4 hours or until firm.

2. Loosen frozen chocolate cubes with thin knife; remove from ice cube trays. Place in blender with remaining ¼ cup milk; pulse to break up chunks. Blend about 30 seconds or until smooth.

FROSTED LEMONADE ▶

MAKES 3 SERVINGS

½ cup sugar
3 cups water, divided
1 cup lemon juice
6 cups vanilla ice cream

1. Combine sugar and ½ cup water in small saucepan; cook over medium-high heat until sugar is dissolved and mixture is clear. Remove from heat; cool slightly.

2. Combine lemon juice, remaining 2½ cups water and sugar syrup in pitcher or large measuring cup. Refrigerate until cold.

3. For each serving, combine 1 cup lemonade and 2 cups ice cream in blender; blend until smooth.

SHAMROCK SHAKE

MAKES 1 SERVING

2 cups low-fat French vanilla ice cream
¼ to ½ cup milk
⅛ teaspoon peppermint extract
10 drops green food coloring
Whipped cream and maraschino cherry (optional)

Combine ice cream, ¼ cup milk, peppermint extract and green food coloring in blender; blend until smooth. Add additional ¼ cup milk, if necessary, to reach desired consistency. Garnish with whipped cream and cherry.

PUMPKIN SPICE LATTE

MAKES 2 SERVINGS

1¾ cups milk, divided

½ cup canned pumpkin

3 tablespoons packed
    brown sugar

1 teaspoon grated
    fresh ginger

1 teaspoon pumpkin pie
    spice

½ teaspoon ground
    cinnamon, plus
    additional for garnish

¼ teaspoon salt

⅛ teaspoon coarsely ground
    black pepper

1 cup strong-brewed
    hot coffee*

1 tablespoon vanilla

Whipped cream (optional)

*Use about 1 tablespoon
ground espresso roast or
other dark roast coffee for
each 3 ounces of water.*

1. Combine ½ cup milk, pumpkin, brown sugar, ginger, pumpkin pie spice, ½ teaspoon cinnamon, salt and pepper in medium saucepan; whisk until well blended. Cook over medium-low heat 10 minutes, whisking frequently.

2. Remove from heat; whisk in coffee and vanilla. Strain through fine-mesh strainer into medium bowl.

3. Bring remaining 1¼ cups milk to a simmer in small saucepan over medium-high heat. For froth, whisk vigorously 30 seconds. Whisk into coffee mixture until blended. Garnish with whipped cream and additional cinnamon.

INSPIRED BY ORANGE JULIUS®

ORANGE WHIP ▸

MAKES 2 SERVINGS

- 2 cups ice cubes
- 1 can (12 ounces) frozen orange juice concentrate with pulp, partially thawed
- 1 cup milk
- ¼ cup powdered sugar
- ½ teaspoon vanilla

Combine ice, orange juice concentrate, milk, powdered sugar and vanilla in blender; pulse to break up ice. Blend until smooth.

INSPIRED BY SONIC®

CHERRY LIMEADE

MAKES 1 SERVING

- Crushed ice
- ¼ lime
- 1 can (12 ounces) lemon-lime soda
- 2 tablespoons thawed frozen limeade concentrate
- 2 tablespoons liquid from maraschino cherry jar
- 1 maraschino cherry (optional)

Fill tall glass with crushed ice. Squeeze lime wedge over ice and drop in lime. Pour soda, limeade and cherry liquid into glass; stir gently. Garnish with maraschino cherry.

CHOCOLATE CAKE MILKSHAKE ▶

MAKES 1 SERVING

1 slice (⅛ of cake)
  Rich Chocolate Cake
  (recipe follows)

½ cup milk

2 scoops vanilla ice cream
  (about 1 cup total)

1. Prepare and frost Rich Chocolate Cake.

2. Combine milk, ice cream and cake slice in blender; blend just until cake is incorporated but texture of shake is not completely smooth.

RICH CHOCOLATE CAKE

MAKES 8 TO 10 SERVINGS

1 package (about 15 ounces)
  devil's food cake mix

1 cup cold water

1 cup mayonnaise

3 eggs

1½ containers (16 ounces
  each) chocolate frosting

1. Preheat oven to 350°F. Spray two 9-inch round cake pans with nonstick cooking spray.

2. Beat cake mix, water, mayonnaise and eggs in large bowl with electric mixer at low speed 30 seconds. Beat at medium speed 2 minutes. Pour batter into prepared pans.

3. Bake about 25 minutes or until toothpick inserted into centers comes out clean. Cool in pans 10 minutes; remove to wire racks to cool completely.

4. Fill and frost cake with chocolate frosting.

PEACH ICED TEA ▶

MAKES 4 SERVINGS

4 cups water
3 black tea bags
¼ cup sugar
1 can (about 11 ounces)
   peach nectar
1 cup frozen peach slices
   Ice cubes

1. Bring water to a boil in medium saucepan over high heat. Remove from heat; add tea bags and let steep 5 minutes. Remove tea bags; stir in sugar until dissolved. Cool to room temperature.

2. Stir in peach nectar and peach slices. Refrigerate until cold. Serve over ice.

beverages

STRAWBERRY LEMONADE

MAKES 5 SERVINGS

3 cups water, divided
1 cup sugar
1 cup frozen strawberries
1½ cups lemon juice

1. Combine 1 cup water, sugar and strawberries in small saucepan; bring to a boil over high heat. Boil 5 minutes. Remove from heat; cool completely.

2. Pour strawberry mixture into blender; blend until smooth. Strain into pitcher. Stir in lemon juice and remaining 2 cups water until blended. Refrigerate until cold.

Another Broken Egg Café®
Turkey Mozzarella Panini, 174

Applebee's® Grill + Bar
Chicken Bacon Quesadillas, 29
Chicken Fajita Roll-Ups, 168
French Quarter Steaks, 212
Shrimp and Spinach Salad, 112
Strawberry Cheesecake Dessert Shooters, 264

Au Bon Pain®
Harvest Pumpkin Soup, 86
Italian Wedding Soup, 94

Bahama Breeze® Island Grille
Island Fish Tacos, 196

Baker's Square® Restaurant & Pies
French Silk Pie, 274

Benihana®
Chicken Fried Rice, 246

Bertucci's® Brick Oven Pizza & Pasta
Lentil Soup, 98
Limoncello Cake with Mascarpone Frosting, 296
Sausage Rice Soup, 104

BJ's Restaurant & Brewhouse®
Garlic Knots, 242
Roasted Brussels Sprouts Salad, 138

Bob Evans® Restaurant
Beef Vegetable Soup, 78

Boston Market®
Cinnamon Apples, 248

Bruegger's Bagels
Garden Vegetable Soup, 96

Buca® di Beppo Italian Restaurant
Cheesy Garlic Bread, 250

Buffalo Wild Wings®
Buffalo Wings, 32

California Pizza Kitchen®
Barbecue Chicken Pizza, 179
BBQ Chicken Salad, 118
Chicken Waldorf Salad, 108
Red Velvet Cake, 280

Carrabba's Italian Grill®
Meatballs and Ricotta, 194
Pasta Campagnolo, 208
Pepperoni Stuffed Mushrooms, 60
Peppery Sicilian Chicken Soup, 90

Cheeseburger in Paradise® Bar & Grill
Cuban Pork Sandwich, 142

The Cheesecake Factory®
Jambalaya Pasta, 218
Pumpkin Cheesecake, 290
Raspberry White Chocolate Cheesecake, 272

Chevy's Fresh Mex®
Classic Flan, 270

Chick-Fil-A®
Frosted Lemonade, 300

Chili's® Grill & Bar
Chicken Enchilada Soup, 74
Guacamole Burgers, 146
Restaurant-Style Baby Back Ribs, 182
Steak Fajitas, 204
White Spinach Queso, 54
Salsa, 58

Chipotle Mexican Grill
Chicken Burrito Bowls, 186
Guacamole, 46

Claim Jumper® Restaurant & Saloon
Meatloaf, 200
Spinach Salad, 134

Cinnabon®
Rich and Gooey Cinnamon Buns, 6

Corner Bakery®
Autumn Harvest Salad, 122
Chicken and Roasted Tomato Panini, 164
Tomato Mozzarella Sandwich, 144

Cracker Barrel® Old Country Store
Classic Macaroni and Cheese, 236

Hearty Hash Brown Casserole, 254

Dairy Queen®
Ice Cream Pizza Treat, 278

Dickey's Barbecue Pit®
Jalapeño Beans, 228

Domino's®
Marbled Cookie Brownie, 266

Fazoli's®
Chicken Parmesan Sliders, 42

First Watch®, The Daytime Cafe
Frittata Rustica, 20
Hearty Veggie Sandwich, 166
Superfood Kale Salad, 130

Hooters®
Buffalo Chicken Dip, 50
Onion Ring Stack, 56
Tex-Mex Nachos, 38

Houlihan's Restaurant and Bar
Smashed Potatoes, 232

Huddle House®
Stuffed Hash Browns, 16

IHOP®
Strawberry Banana French Toast, 12
Strawberry-Topped Pancakes, 24

Jason's Deli®
Great Reuben Sandwich, The, 170
New Orleans-Style Muffaletta, 162

Joe's Crab Shack®
Crab Shack Dip, 62

Lone Star Steakhouse
Wedge Salad, 107

Longhorn® Steakhouse
Bourbon-Marinated Salmon, 184

KFC®
Coleslaw, 221

Maggiano's Little Italy®
Zucchini Fritte, 48

Margaritaville®
Key Lime Pie, 260

Marie Callender's® Restaurant & Bakery
Banana Cream Pie, 284
Simple Golden Corn Bread, 234

McAlister's® Deli
Vegetarian Chili, 88

McDonald's®
Shamrock Shake, 300

Morton's™ The Steakhouse
Carrot Cake, 286
Steakhouse Chopped Salad, 116

Nando's® Peri-Peri Chicken
Peri-Peri Chicken, 192

Noodles & Company®
Pesto Cavatappi, 214

Olive Garden® Italian Kitchen
Brownie Lasagna, 288
Bruschetta, 52
Chicken and Gnocchi Soup, 100
Chicken Marsala, 206
Classic Lasagna, 202
Eggplant Parmesan, 190
Fettuccine Alfredo, 180
Hearty Tuscan Soup, 72
House Salad, 120
Minestrone Soup, 80
Pasta Fagioli, 84
Peach Iced Tea, 308
Soft Garlic Breadsticks, 222
Spinach-Artichoke Dip, 34
Tiramisu, 268
Toasted Ravioli, 44
Warm Apple Crostata, 258

Orange Julius®
Orange Whip, 304

The Original® Pancake House
Baked Apple Pancake, 18
Dutch Baby Pancake, 5

Outback Steakhouse®
Aussie Chicken, 216
Big Onion, The, 36

Broccoli and Cheese, 240
Chocolate Storm, 257
Coconut Shrimp, 210
Double Chocolate Cookies and Cream Mousse, 282
Loaded Baked Potatoes, 224

Panera Bread®
Almond Chicken Salad Sandwich, 152
Amazing Apple Salad, 136
Broccoli Cheese Soup, 69
Creamy Tomato Soup, 92
Green Goddess Cobb Salad, 110
Mediterranean Vegetable Sandwich, 160
Southwest Turkey Sandwich, 148
Strawberry Poppy Seed Chicken Salad, 126
Tuna Salad Sandwich, 172
Spinach Artichoke Egg Soufflés, 10

Pappadeaux® Seafood Kitchen
Sweet Potato Pecan Pie, 294

Pei Wei®
Bangkok Peanut Noodles, 198
Hot and Sour Soup, 102

P.F. Chang's®
Chicken Lettuce Wraps, 64
Mongolian Beef, 188

Popeyes®
Cajun Rice, 252
Spicy Chicken Sandwich, 176

Portillo's®
Chocolate Cake Milkshake, 306
Chocolate Eclair Cake, 292
Garbage Salad, 132
Rich Chocolate Cake, 306

Potbelly Sandwich Shop®
Mediterranean Salad, 124

Red Lobster®
Cheddar Biscuits, 230
Hush Puppies, 238

Red Robin®
Classic Patty Melts, 158
Strawberry Lemonade, 308

Ruth's Chris® Steakhouse
Brussels Sprouts with Honey Butter, 244
Steakhouse Creamed Spinach, 226

Snooze® an A.M. Eatery
Sweet Potato Pancakes, 8

Sonic®
Cherry Limeade, 304

Starbucks®
Cinnamon Swirl Coffeecake, 14
Glazed Lemon Loaf, 276
Pumpkin Bread, 26
Pumpkin Spice Latte, 302

Taco Bell®
Double Decker Tacos, 154

TGI Fridays℠
Black Bean Soup, 70
Classic French Onion Soup, 82
Mozzarella Sticks, 30
Pecan-Crusted Chicken Salad, 114
Potato Skins, 40
Spinach Florentine Flatbread, 66
Toffee Cake with Whiskey Sauce, 262
Tuscan Portobello Melt, 141

Tony Roma's®
Baked Potato Soup, 76

Waffle House®
Pecan Waffles, 22

Wendy's®
Chocolate Frosty, 299
Taco Salad Supreme, 128

Which Wich®? Superior Sandwiches
BLT Supreme, 150

Yard House®
Blackened Chicken Torta, 156

VOLUME MEASUREMENTS (dry)

⅛ teaspoon = 0.5 mL
¼ teaspoon = 1 mL
½ teaspoon = 2 mL
¾ teaspoon = 4 mL
1 teaspoon = 5 mL
1 tablespoon = 15 mL
2 tablespoons = 30 mL
¼ cup = 60 mL
⅓ cup = 75 mL
½ cup = 125 mL
⅔ cup = 150 mL
¾ cup = 175 mL
1 cup = 250 mL
2 cups = 1 pint = 500 mL
3 cups = 750 mL
4 cups = 1 quart = 1 L

VOLUME MEASUREMENTS (fluid)

1 fluid ounce (2 tablespoons) = 30 mL
4 fluid ounces (½ cup) = 125 mL
8 fluid ounces (1 cup) = 250 mL
12 fluid ounces (1½ cups) = 375 mL
16 fluid ounces (2 cups) = 500 mL

WEIGHTS (mass)

½ ounce = 15 g
1 ounce = 30 g
3 ounces = 90 g
4 ounces = 120 g
8 ounces = 225 g
10 ounces = 285 g
12 ounces = 360 g
16 ounces = 1 pound = 450 g

DIMENSIONS

1/16 inch = 2 mm
⅛ inch = 3 mm
¼ inch = 6 mm
½ inch = 1.5 cm
¾ inch = 2 cm
1 inch = 2.5 cm

OVEN TEMPERATURES

250°F = 120°C
275°F = 140°C
300°F = 150°C
325°F = 160°C
350°F = 180°C
375°F = 190°C
400°F = 200°C
425°F = 220°C
450°F = 230°C

BAKING PAN SIZES

Utensil	Size in Inches/Quarts	Metric Volume	Size in Centimeters
Baking or Cake Pan (square or rectangular)	8×8×2	2 L	20×20×5
	9×9×2	2.5 L	23×23×5
	12×8×2	3 L	30×20×5
	13×9×2	3.5 L	33×23×5
Loaf Pan	8×4×3	1.5 L	20×10×7
	9×5×3	2 L	23×13×7
Round Layer Cake Pan	8×1½	1.2 L	20×4
	9×1½	1.5 L	23×4
Pie Plate	8×1¼	750 mL	20×3
	9×1¼	1 L	23×3
Baking Dish or Casserole	1 quart	1 L	—
	1½ quart	1.5 L	—
	2 quart	2 L	—